HOUSTON LOST AND UNBUILT

★

Roger Fullington Series in Architecture

HOUSTON
LOST AND UNBUILT

★

STEVEN R. STROM

UNIVERSITY OF TEXAS PRESS ⟨⟩ AUSTIN

Publication of this book was made possible in part by support from Roger Fullington and a challenge grant from the National Endowment for the Humanities.

Requests for permission to reproduce material from this work should be sent to:
  Permissions
  University of Texas Press
  P.O. Box 7819
  Austin, TX 78713-7819
  www.utexas.edu/utpress/about/bpermission.html

⊗ The paper used in this book meets the minimum requirements of
ANSI/NISO Z39.48-1992 (R1997) (Permanence of Paper).

Library of Congress Cataloging-in-Publication Data

Strom, Steven.
  Houston lost and unbuilt / Steven R. Strom. — 1st ed.
    p.   cm. — (Roger Fullington series in architecture)
  Includes bibliographical references and index.
  ISBN 978-0-292-72113-5 (cloth : alk. paper)
  1. Lost architecture—Texas—Houston.   2. Unbuilt architectural projects—
Texas—Houston.   3. Houston (Tex.)—Buildings, structures, etc.   I. Title.
  NA735.H68S77   2010
  720.9764′1411—dc22
                                          2009017503

CONTENTS

★

THE INSPIRATION TO write this book resulted from the reactions to the publication of two articles that I wrote for *Cite: The Architecture and Design Magazine of Houston*. The first article, "Lost Houston: Images From a Century of Erasure," appeared in the Fall 1999/Winter 2000 issue of *Cite*. Shortly after the article appeared, I began to receive responses—first e-mails and phone calls and then, unbelievably, handwritten letters. Eventually, several dozen people had contacted me, and almost every single one of them responded with the same basic message: seeing images of Houston buildings that they had known so well in their past, now destroyed and lost forever, had generated an overwhelming, palpable sense of loss. Rather than simply feeling nostalgic, however, many of the readers noted that for the first time they felt true anger at seeing visible proof of the poor job that Houston had done in saving its architectural heritage. Perhaps it was the number of photos and architectural drawings in the article or simply the combination of images that generated such a response . . . who knows? Nonetheless, these people felt compelled to respond in an age when few have the time to express their thoughts over something as seemingly inconsequential as a magazine article. Clearly something had struck a nerve in the consciousness of these Houstonians.

With the subsequent publication of another article, "The Houston that Never Was" (Spring 2001), there was again an unexpected number of responses from readers. There is a long-standing tradition in architectural circles to fantasize about buildings that reached the conceptual stage but were never completed. My article pointed out that some purely conceptual Houston projects might be the better for never having been completed in terms of aesthetics and potential negative social and environmental impact. Alternatively, the city was poorer due to its failure to complete other building projects. The people writing and calling about this later article also expressed strong opinions, commenting that it had made them think in new ways about these unbuilt projects. The article made such an impression on architects and preservationists that copies were sometimes handed out on architectural tours, and one professor even made it required reading for one of his architecture classes. As a result of the positive feedback that I received regarding both articles, I decided to increase the number of illustrations of both lost buildings and unbuilt projects and combine them into a single book. In addition, during the course of my research, I realized that the category of "lost" needed to be expanded to include interiors and store display windows. Fortunately, University of Texas Press ultimately accepted my proposal and the result follows.

I have purposely chosen to concentrate only on civic and commercial structures during the period from the beginning of the twentieth century to the early years of the twenty-first century. Expanding the book to include domestic architecture would have been too massive a project, although this area is certainly worthy of future research. *Houston's Forgotten Heritage*, published in 1991, covered the city's local domestic architecture so thoroughly up to the beginning of World War I that it deserves a companion piece focusing on the remainder of the twentieth century. Similarly, I did not cover lost structures in the Hispanic community because Dr. Thomas Kreneck documented them so well in his 1989 study *Del Pueblo: A Pictorial History of Houston's Hispanic Community*. Author David Welling has also done a wonderful job of chronicling Houston movie theaters patronized by Hispanics in *Cinema Houston*. Despite these omissions, the photos included in the book reveal an architectural toll that is inconceivable. It is my hope that this book's audience will be moved to help salvage Houston's remaining historic architecture.

I have provided some background history to accompany the photographs and drawings, but the images are the real stars of this book. None of the captions were ever intended to be in-depth histories of the lost structures or of the architects who built them. However, even if I had wanted the captions to provide more of this information, this task might have proven to be impossible. Despite the volume of information available about Houston's lost architecture, there is still a surprising deficit of original historical resources. The City of Houston did not preserve even the most basic construction and building permit records until the 1970s when some city departments began a semi-concerted effort to do so. The laissez-faire attitude shown by municipal departments toward history was a direct reflection of the almost total disinterest shown by the general populace; only in the past twenty to twenty-five years have Houstonians shown any interest toward historic preservation. The percentage of the city's total population that could be considered preservation activists remains dismally small, but they represent a vocal, organized, well-educated, and increasingly influential minority.

Assembling this book was incredibly fun for me. The photos sometimes presented intriguing cases that called for extensive detective work to unlock the mysteries of Houston's lost past. The observer must scan each photo for visual clues revealing details about its proper placement in time and space. I particularly enjoyed piecing together the visual clues contained in the photograph of the Iris Theatre. The film title on the marquee, *Courtin' Wildcats*, dates the photo to 1929, but further inspection provided clues that allowed me to set a more specific date. First, Christmas lights are strung along the theater's façade. Granted, many entertainment venues used colored lights for decoration in the 1920s, so it was possible that these were not Christmas lights after all. However, one can see that Christmas trees are for sale in the lower left-hand corner of the picture, so the photograph was definitely taken at Christmastime. Second, remains of ice and slush are visible along the curb. According to the National Weather Service, Houston had a fair-sized snowstorm on December 22, 1929. Combining this information with the date of the featured film's debut made it possible to date the photo within an accuracy of a few days.

Initially, I tried a number of ways to organize and group the photographs, including by date of construc-

tion, by decade, or by building type (commercial, civic, etc.), but none of these groupings proved to be very successful in terms of the impression that I was trying to make. In the end, I maintained the order of the original "Lost Houston" article. Several readers of the article commented that they liked the "random" way the photos were presented. As they reviewed the photographs, the appearance of, for example, a department store, followed by a church, followed by a government building gave them a better impression of the full range of the destruction of Houston's architectural legacy. In cases in which architectural obliteration was more pronounced, photos were grouped thematically, such as by building type (e.g., theaters) or physical area (Fourth Ward/Freedmen's Town).

All of the architectural drawings reproduced in this book came from collections housed in the Architectural Archive of the Houston Public Library's Houston Metropolitan Research Center (HMRC). The majority of the photographs used in the book also came from HMRC's photo collections, although some photos from the Bob Bailey Studio Photographic Archives, housed at the University of Texas's Center for American History (CAH) were also used.

I extend my appreciation to Don Carleton, CAH Executive Director, and Linda Peterson, Head of Photographic and Digital Archives at CAH, for allowing me to use the Bailey photo archives prior to the cataloging of the collection. It is noteworthy that it was an Austin institution that saved the Bob Bailey Collection from almost certain destruction by neglect and lack of preservation funds during the time the collection was stored in Houston. Not a single Houston library or museum came up with funds to maintain the Bailey photos, a collection of national and even world importance, in the city that the Bailey Studio chronicled for decades.

Much of the research for the book was completed using the vertical files of HMRC's Architectural Archive and Texas Room, which contain a wealth of information about Houston's history. Thanks go to the HMRC staff, particularly Tammy Jordan, archivist; Joel Draut, photo archivist; and Billy Hoya, library assistant. Mark Carley provided his excellent editorial and organizational skills while I was writing the manuscript. Jim Burr, my editor at University of Texas Press, was patient, supportive, and extremely helpful throughout the entire production process. Manuscript editor Victoria Davis, also with UT

Press, is responsible for making the text readable. Mitchell Shields, former editor of *Cite* magazine, is due credit for using his formidable editorial skills to hone each of my articles that appeared in that magazine, making my text more effective in the process.

Credit also goes to Bob, Martha, and Maude Bauer of Austin and Houston for providing clippings from their personal collection that gave new insights into Houston's futuristic thinking. In addition, photographer Eric Hamburg of Redondo Beach, California showed his usual high level of skills in photographing some of the images in this book that did not have existing negatives. However, I owe perhaps the most to architect Barry Moore, who taught me how to look at architecture in new and exciting ways.

AUTHOR'S NOTE

MUCH OF THE HISTORICAL information used in the photograph captions of *Houston: Lost and Unbuilt* was obtained from the clippings, photographs, pamphlets, and other ephemera contained in the vertical files of the Architectural Archive, Houston Metropolitan Research Center (HMRC). Although I also used a separate collection of vertical files housed in HMRC's Texas Room, these files understandably did not contain the same breadth of information about Houston's built environment as the architectural files.

The downside to the wealth of historical information contained in the vertical files is that documentation of original sources for file materials is often spotty at best. As the files were added to over the years, uncataloged photos, undated newspaper clippings from unidentified newspapers, and other miscellaneous, sometimes mysterious, pieces of information found their way into the files. The chronological range of the files—the whole of the twentieth century and the initial years of the twenty-first—coupled with a large staff turnover through the years guaranteed that there was often scant knowledge regarding the sources of many items contained in HMRC's vertical files.

Because I used many thousands of items from these files, I have opted to list the titles of the vertical files when identifying their contents as source material. The files are also listed as simply being from HMRC rather than the Houston Public Library's Architectural Archive, because the Architectural Archive was subsumed under the broader mantle of HMRC. The previously separate collection of architectural vertical files is now integrated into HMRC's other holdings.

The sheer volume of Houston historical information contained in these vertical files is staggering. Unfortu-nately, the files have not received proper care, in terms of both preservation and physical security. Many items have gone "missing" from HMRC's vertical files in recent years, and, as of this writing, no reliable methods have been instituted to guard any of the HMRC's other materials: maps, files, books, photographs, manuscript collections, and drawings.

In 1996, I attended a lecture by an archivist from the Netherlands who issued a rousing call for all libraries and archives to toss their vertical files into the nearest trash bin—with the dawn of the Internet, materials of the sort contained in vertical files were now a vestige of the pre–World Wide Web era. This book is a testament to the fallacy of this kind of thinking.

During the course of my research, I also employed the Architectural Archive's collection of full-scale architectural drawings and, of course, the HMRC's extensive photographic collections. In addition, I was extremely fortunate to be able to use the Bob Bailey Studio Photographic Collection shortly after its acquisition by the Center for American History at the University of Texas. At the time, my research consisted of looking through boxes of uncataloged, disarranged files of negatives recently moved from Houston in their original condition. Since that time, the Center for American History has provided every researcher of Houston's history (and the history of photography, for that matter) a tremendous service by expeditiously cataloging a large portion of the Bob Bailey Collection and even making many of the photos available online. Every Houstonian owes the Center for American History a debt of gratitude for its acquisition, preservation, and organization of Bob Bailey's photographs.

HOUSTON LOST AND UNBUILT

★

I

LOST

HOUSTON

INTRODUCTION

*"[T]here can be no history where there
are no memories to hold on to."*
—REINALDO ARENAS, CUBAN POET

*"Remove not the ancient landmark,
which thy fathers have set."*
—PROVERBS 23:28

THIS BOOK WAS WRITTEN with one primary purpose in mind: to impart some idea of the loss and disruption that has been inflicted on the residents of Houston, Texas, by the steady and systematic destruction of the city's built environment over the past century. If the tone of this book is elegiac, it is meant to be. The range of buildings that have been destroyed is remarkable in its scope, and the toll on Houston's citizens has at times bordered on an almost spiritual or psychic level of loss. The photographs and architectural drawings that accompany this essay chronicle a city that entered the twentieth century in a semi-rural state to emerge on the dawn of the twenty-first century as a vast sea of concrete scattered with only a few remaining buildings from the early decades of the previous century.[1] The destruction of buildings on this scale has been seen before as the result of massive wars; in Houston, however, the pursuit of money and the new and "modern" has had an almost as devastating effect on the city's built environment as World War II had on cities such as Berlin, Warsaw, and Tokyo. A radical and isolating disconnection has occurred in Houston between the past and the present.

Maintaining a sense of place, of being able to relate to the built environment, is one of the primary factors in imparting a sense of community and citizenship among the residents of a city. Unfortunately, the tendency of Houston's government has often been to make it easy for developers to demolish older structures deemed commercially unviable. Consequently, no visible traces remain if nostalgic Houstonians wish to visit their childhood neighborhoods, schools, restaurants, stores, or churches. Bruce Webb's description of Houston as the "Ephemeral City" has provided us with the best analogy for the city's urban condition: here today, gone tomorrow.[2] In addition, the very auto-oriented transportation network that contributes so much to Houston's commercial stature creates the ever-expanding, outward growth patterns that move people away from the original urban core, ultimately contributing to the economic factors that make it easier to demolish a building than to restore and adaptively reuse it. Reinaldo Arenas's description of Miami as "not really a city but rather a number of detached houses peopled by cowboys for whom the horse had been replaced by the car" could be applied with equal accuracy to Houston's general lack of binding communal feelings and absence of genuine urbanity.[3]

In short, the city's power brokers have eradicated so much of the built environment that it has become increasingly difficult for many residents to not feel some sort of emotional isolation and dislocation from the city that they call home. Sensing this distance, many urban historians and critics have commented that Houston offers no coherent sense of being a viable, functioning metropolis. The dislocation of the city's residents is often misinterpreted as dislike for the city, when in fact it is oftentimes just the opposite. Many Houstonians want badly to relate to and identify with Houston's urban environment, but the rapid and wholesale loss of the city's architectural fabric increasingly makes this almost impossible and results in this restless sense of anomie.

Historian Simon Winchester, writing about San Francisco in the aftermath of the 1906 earthquake, describes why cities that are devastated by disasters are able to not only recover from immediate damage, but also thrive

Satsuma orange grove. A record-shattering freeze in 1895 put an end to any hopes that Houston would be able to compete with Florida and California as a major producer of citrus fruit. Nonetheless, thousands of acres of fruit groves continued to exist in the Houston area for many years to serve local markets. Citrus, pear, peach, and fig orchards remained in operation well into the twentieth century, sometimes only a few miles from downtown. (MSS 187-275, Courtesy HMRC, Houston Public Library.)

Rice harvesting. The rural quality of early twentieth-century Houston is shown in this photo of farmers hauling rice in fields near the city. As late as the 1960s, huge swaths of land surrounding Houston's metropolitan area were devoted to farming and ranching. Although still grown commercially nearby, rice and other agricultural products have only a fraction of the importance they once held in Houston's economic output. (MSS 187-280, Courtesy HMRC, Houston Public Library.)

*Early twentieth century scene of stream near Houston. This photograph was probably taken in the 1920s. It provides an excellent view of the lush, semitropical foliage that once occupied the banks of local bayous and waterways everywhere around and within the city. Wild areas such as this were easily accessible from any part of the city in the early decades of the twentieth century. Today the number of large parcels of natural areas adjacent to Houston have virtually disappeared, a byproduct not merely of urbanization but also of the channelizing of local waterways to prevent flooding. A radical disconnect with the natural environment has taken place in the lives of most Houstonians, who once had easy access to pastoral scenes like this. (*MSS 157-73, Courtesy *HMRC, Houston Public Library.)*

and prosper once again. In *A Crack In the Edge of the World*, Winchester notes that the recovery of these cities is based on "reasons that go far beyond the accumulation of buildings that is their outward manifestation." The qualities that inspire the citizens of such cities to remain and rebuild rather than pack up and relocate are "invariably due to some combination of geography and climate, together with some vague and indefinable organic reason that persuades mankind to settle there."[4]

Should a catastrophic disaster strike Houston, there is no doubt in my mind that the city—humidity, insects, heat, and all—would rebuild and reconstitute itself on a grand scale. However, no one would claim that Houston has any "combination of geography and climate" that would motivate its citizens to rebuild— quite the opposite. The frequently miserable conditions of Houston's semitropical climate are well known. And the flat bleakness of much of the Gulf Coast prairie on which Houston is built inspires little more than a feeling of monotony. And yet, millions of people call Houston home and have tremendous love and affection for the city. Perhaps this can be chalked up to what Winchester would call a "vague and indefinable organic reason." Some would argue, however, that the reason Houston would survive a catastrophe is quite clear and definable: commerce. It is true that commerce, along with the jobs it provides, continues to be the primary factor that draws new arrivals to Houston. And, commerce would engender reconstruction were the city to suffer a major catastrophe. But commerce alone does not create loyalty to a place, and the successes of virtually unbridled capitalism offer no complete explanation for the emotional bonds that so many Houstonians have with their city.

Despite the fact that Houston entered the twenty-first century as the nation's fourth largest city, the rest of the United States has little sense of its identity except that it

Automobile accident, 1912. Photographer Frank Schlueter took this photograph following a car accident in South Houston. The picture provides an excellent example of just how rural Houston's immediate environs were less than a century ago. The photo also points to the incredible rate at which transportation in Houston, along with the rest of the country, became mechanized, for it was most likely the sheer novelty of the wrecked car that caused Schlueter to shoot the image in the first place. By the end of the next decade, Houston's streets were often the scenes of immense traffic jams. (MSS 157-54, Courtesy HMRC, Houston Public Library.)

is inextricably linked to a fanatical hunger for modernity and the new.[5] That Americans have a penchant for the newest and/or the most modern in every facet of life—particularly in the area of technological innovations—is hardly a startling revelation. But few cities of any size, certainly no city the size of Houston, have gone about the search for modernity with such zeal. Even Los Angeles, known nationwide for its poor track record for architectural preservation, has salvaged more of its past than Houston. Houstonians followed the exhortation of cultural modernists to "Make it new," and although "new" and "modern" are not necessarily synonymous, by the mid-twentieth century, for all practical purposes, they were one and the same in Houston. In 1976, *New York Times* architecture critic Ada Louise Huxtable (in)famously labeled Houston as *the* "city of the second half of the Twentieth Century," a moniker that Houston never failed—or even attempted to fail—to live up

to.[6] Huxtable was, of course, largely referring to the important Postmodernist structures, such as the Pennzoil Building, that were being built around Houston at the time. Huxtable attributed much of this architecturally innovative spirit to Houston's lack of zoning regulations. Whether this was correct or not, the same failure to impose some form of genuine urban planning has resulted in the obliteration of much of the city's past and the rapid spread of horrific urban sprawl.

Houston's unfaltering adherence to modernity went hand in hand with a boundless faith in the future, along with the certainty that modernity cloaked the city with an aura of progressivism. The consequence of that crusade for modernity has been the destruction of the city's past, both distant and more recent. At the beginning of the twenty-first century, even many of the great Modernist buildings that had built Houston's nationwide reputation in the mid-century for being on the cutting

Main Street at Buffalo Bayou, 1910. This is another photograph by Frank Schlueter, showing the foot of Main Street at Buffalo Bayou. Because this port scene was photographed prior to the completion of the Houston Ship Channel in 1914, with the exception of some of the newer buildings in the background, it looks scarcely different than it would have at the time of the Civil War. (MSS 157-58, Courtesy HMRC, Houston Public Library.)

Flood damage, Buffalo Bayou, 1935. Showing the aftermath of the disastrous flood of December 1935, this photo clearly conveys the degree to which Houston was largely at the mercy of natural forces until the channelizing and concreting of local waterways was completed by the mid-twentieth century. (MSS 157-1095, Courtesy HMRC, Houston Public Library.)

edge of architectural innovation are in danger of being destroyed, scarcely five decades after their construction. It is the great paradox of modernity that progress is simultaneously accompanied by destruction. Many Houstonians are finally becoming aware of the consummate irony of modernity: that by the very definition of modernism, a newly completed building, freeway, subdivision, or mall is already outdated at the very moment of completion.

Advocating the new is not automatically accompanied by an improvement in the quality of life. In Houston, more often than not, this focus on the new has actually led to a notable decline in the quality of life. No matter how much criticism is levied against urban conditions in Los Angeles (the American city that is possibly the

most comparable to Houston in its similarities and excesses), it is a real city. It has the features that provide a quality of life missing in Houston: a viable downtown, neighborhoods containing both the basic necessities and amenities for urban living, and a reasonably organic pattern of growth. And despite its own carelessness with the preservation of its past, Los Angeles most definitely has a history, apparent in the many historic buildings that remain a part of the city's daily fabric.

As the new century begins, more and more Houstonians are beginning to realize the consequences of their inaction over the years as, increasingly, beloved landmarks or neighborhoods are becoming endangered. The mere persistence of memory cannot begin to compensate for the loss of an actual structure. At some point, Hous-

Houston skyline, ca. 1950. The downtown Houston skyline as seen from the roof of the Jefferson Davis Hospital, ca. 1950. The San Felipe Courts public housing project (later Allen Parkway Village) is in the foreground. In less than five decades Houston was transformed from a muddy, sleepy, backwater town into the largest city in the South. (Jefferson Davis Hospital (1939) Vertical File, Courtesy HMRC, Houston Public Library.)

tonians must halt their fixation with newness and begin to hold on to some of their architectural memories, if not for themselves then at least for their descendants. Only then will Houston have even a chance of becoming a great city. The greatness of a city is not measured by the number of its sport venues or by attendance at public festivals. By sacrificing its architectural past, including the immediate past, Houston has placed itself in a historical void that makes the city neither comforting to longtime residents, nor particularly interesting to new arrivals.

I am not suggesting that Houstonians can overthrow modernity as a way of life, but they should not be held hostage by it. Despite numerous pronouncements of the death of modernity, it is still the driving force that operates our national, and most of the world's, culture.

Advocating the abandonment of modernity would not only be foolish and utopian, it would also be impossible. I am simply suggesting that in the very near future there must be some partial halt to Houston's quest for modernity, long enough to save what little is left of its past. The combination of futurism and a feverish desire to embrace technology has resulted in the massive destruction of every conceivable building type, leading to serious feelings of loss for many Houstonians who are already struggling to adapt to an ever-changing urban landscape as well as the daily stresses caused by ever-accelerating modernity.

While I was writing this introduction, Houston was abuzz with the news that three more of the city's historic Art Deco structures would soon face the possibility of destruction: the 1939 Alabama Theatre, partially preserved and still used as a bookstore; a portion of the pathbreaking 1937 River Oaks Shopping Center; and the River Oaks Theatre, also completed in 1939 and, amazingly, still operating as a movie house. The press, both local and national, was full of optimism that this time a nerve has been struck, and that at last Houstonians would not allow the demolitions to take place. Thousands of people signed petitions, spoke before the city council, wrote letters, and demonstrated their displeasure in a variety of ways. All of these actions were taken as proof that this time it would be different. And yet, with historical hindsight it all seems so familiar. It could be the 3,000-strong demonstration by preservationists who marched around the Shamrock Hotel in 1987 in a futile effort to save that historic structure. Or, it could be the thousands of people who protested the planned destruction of the Village Theatre, which was demolished in 1994. Each decade, it seems, there are architectural causes to rally around, and often the results have been far from encouraging for preservationists. Despite my hope that this time would be different and that the developers would not win this go-around, by the time I completed my manuscript the River Oaks Shopping Center was partially demolished and the Alabama and River Oaks theaters remained in danger.

Many of the lost buildings highlighted in these photographs share one characteristic. They were "public" buildings, in the broadest sense of that word. While some of these lost structures were actually civic, and therefore built to be public buildings, others—theaters, hotels, and department stores, for example—were also used by hundreds of thousands of Houstonians. As a result, they became repositories of shared, public experiences and knowledge. The successors to these irreplaceable structures have generally failed to impart the same sense of *communitas* among Houston's populace, particularly when the successor turns out to be a parking garage or surface parking lot. Hopefully, this survey of lost buildings will also teach people to look at everyday structures with a different outlook and not to dismiss or take for

granted so-called "mundane" commercial and industrial buildings. As one of the photos shows, even a building so seemingly banal as the local Pepsi-Cola bottling plant generates shared memories for thousands of people.

The illustrations that follow will give the reader some idea of the enormous losses that Houston's heritage has suffered in little more than a century. The buildings memorialized in this book represent only a small sample of what Houston has lost. Perhaps seeing these images will inspire some people not only to remember bits of their bygone past, but also to help prevent similar losses of our history in the future. Such an effort is not simply an exercise in shopworn nostalgia; we are talking about the preservation of structures that are actually extant and not fantastic, like Disneyland's Main Street. Houston, contrary to what many people believe, does have a history. This past is primarily present in an ever-shrinking number of endangered buildings. Only a massive collective effort by the public can save the remainder of Houston's architectural and historical past.

NOTES

1. For a discussion of the importance of agriculture in late-nineteenth and early-twentieth century Houston, see Nancy Hadley and Steven R. Strom, "Innovation, Boosterism, and Agriculture on the Gulf Coast, 1890–1920."

2. Webb, "The Name Game."

3. Arenas, *Before Night Falls*.

4. Winchester, pp. 302–303.

5. Throughout the text, I have lowercased "modern" when discussing a contemporary era and its characteristics and capitalized "Modern" when identifying an architectural style. For the sake of simplicity, I am defining "modern" as a nineteenth-century concept, derived from the philosophies of the Enlightenment, in which for the first time humans became future oriented and began to place an almost religious faith in the processes of both progress and change. The institutionalization of progress and change was accompanied by a limitless optimism that the future would always be better than the present and that change for the sake of change was always good.

6. Huxtable, 1976.

— Houston Municipal Auditorium —

FEW ARCHITECTS or architectural historians have ever bemoaned the demolition of the Houston Municipal Auditorium, more commonly known as the City Auditorium. Architect Barry Moore described it as an "old, unlovely and unloved white elephant" at the time of its destruction in the 1960s. Completed in 1910, the Municipal Auditorium was notable for being the first large Houston commission for the St. Louis firm of Mauran & Russell, who would go on to build the second incarnation of the Rice Hotel two years later.

Although squat and stolid in appearance, the City Auditorium, located on the block now occupied by the Jesse H. Jones Hall for the Performing Arts, was one of Houston's most important civic structures for over half of a century. The auditorium's longevity, combined with the innumerable plays, concerts, conventions, Christmas parties, and other functions that were held there made a distinct impression on the collective unconscious of many Houstonians during the first half of the twentieth century. The artists who performed in the City Auditorium ranged from Enrico Caruso, to Marian Anderson, to Judy Garland.

With the passage of time, many people who fondly remembered attending events in the City Auditorium glossed over the building's less-attractive qualities, such as it often being bitterly cold in the winter and suffocatingly hot during Houston's long summers. The entire structure was demolished in 1963 to make way for Jones Hall, which opened in 1966.

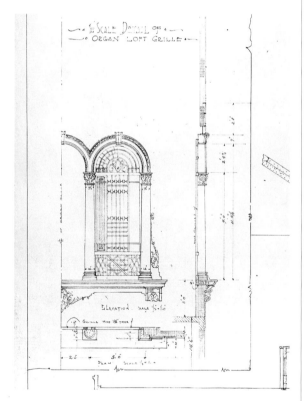

Organ loft detail, Mauran & Russell. (MSS 19-Job 332, Alfred Finn Collection, Courtesy HMRC, Houston Public Library.)

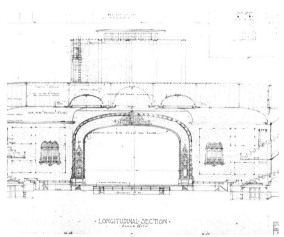

Longitudinal section drawing of auditorium stage. (MSS 19-Job 332, Alfred Finn Collection, Courtesy HMRC, Houston Public Library.)

New curtain for the City Auditorium designed by Alfred Finn, 1925. (MSS 19-840, Alfred Finn Collection, Courtesy HMRC, Houston Public Library.)

Detail of curtain drawing for the City Auditorium, January, 1925. The allegorical representation of the City of Houston looks more like a contemporary 1920s flapper than a goddess from the classical past. (MSS 19-1357, Alfred Finn Collection, Courtesy HMRC, Houston Public Library.)

View of City Auditorium soon after completion in 1910. (MSS 114-660, Courtesy HMRC, Houston Public Library.)

Like many of Houston's buildings in the late nineteenth and early twentieth centuries, the City Auditorium was depicted on postcards. (MSS 187-255, Courtesy HMRC, Houston Public Library.)

The Jesse Jones Hall for the Performing Arts, completed in 1966, occupies the former site of the City Auditorium. Jones Hall represents one of the few instances in Houston's architectural history when a demolished building's successor outshone the original structure. (MSS 157-354, Courtesy HMRC, Houston Public Library.)

Democratic National Convention Hall (Sam Houston Hall)

In 1928, HOUSTON financier Jesse H. Jones stunned cities that had traditionally held national political party conventions, such as Chicago and Baltimore, by helping Houston to win the right to hold the Democratic Party's convention that year. In part an attempt by party leaders to mollify its Southern constituents, who were sure to be displeased by the pending nomination of New York governor Al Smith, it would be the first time since the Civil War that a Southern city hosted a national political convention. Although Houston had no facility large enough to host such a gathering, Jones promised the Democratic National Committee that a

new auditorium would be completed in time for the June convention. Construction began on the Democratic National Convention Hall, known formally as Sam Houston Hall, on March 26 and was completed in only sixty-four days at a cost of some $200,000. Designed by architect Kenneth Franzheim, who became Houston's principal commercial architect after World War II, the auditorium had seating for 16,000 people and its floor space covered approximately six acres. Jones claimed that one million feet of long-leaf yellow pine was utilized in the building's construction.

Aside from the fact that the hall was completed in

The nearly completed, lamella-type framework of the Democratic National Convention Hall's roof is visible in this photo taken during the building's construction in 1928. (MSS 19-1347, Courtesy HMRC, Houston Public Library.)

The nearly completed Convention Hall, May 12, 1928. W. A. Dowdy, who is listed as an architect along with Kenneth Franzheim on the lower left of the photo, served as the architect for the City of Houston and acted as on-site consultant during construction. (MSS 100-941, Courtesy HMRC, Houston Public Library.)

record time, it also showcased an engineering innovation—a lamella-type roof. The construction was overseen by John W. Link's Lamella Trussless Roof Company. (Amazingly, Link's home, built in 1911, still stands on Montrose Boulevard.) The lamella roof-framing process, devised in Europe only a few years earlier, used standardized pieces of lumber curved on one side and beveled on both ends. The pieces of lumber are then joined in crosspieces to create a diamond-patterned, curved roof. In an effort to provide the delegates with unimpeded views, the interior of the Convention Hall contained only twelve columns. Consequently, the roof basically served as the building's framework. Since the lamella roofing process could also be used to build a circular roof, it is possible that the Democratic National Convention Hall may have been an inspiration for the construction of the Harris County Domed Stadium, which used steel beams in a similar process.

The Democratic National Convention took place during June 26–28, 1928, and giant "typhoon" fans were installed to provide sufficient air circulation. However, many of the delegates must have remembered Houston's summer climate for decades after they returned home because the Democrats did not hold another convention in the South until 1972, when Miami was selected as the host city.

Jesse H. Jones (right), the Houston businessman responsible for ensuring that Houston was selected as the site of the 1928 Democratic National Convention, personally inspects the Convention Hall's lamella roofing during construction. Jones would later become the head of the Reconstruction Finance Corporation during the Great Depression and secretary of commerce in Franklin Roosevelt's cabinet. The middle-class housing that still occupied much of the present-day downtown area can be seen in the background. (MSS 157-358, Courtesy HMRC, Houston Public Library.)

Jesse H. Jones (left) reviews architectural plans during an on-site inspection of the Convention Hall. (MSS 19-1345, Courtesy Houston Metropolitan Research Center, Houston Public Library.)

The newly completed Convention Hall, June 1928. (MSS 114-2138, Courtesy HMRC, Houston Public Library.)

Convention delegates in session, June 26–28, 1928. (Democratic Convention Hall Vertical File, Courtesy HMRC, Houston Public Library.)

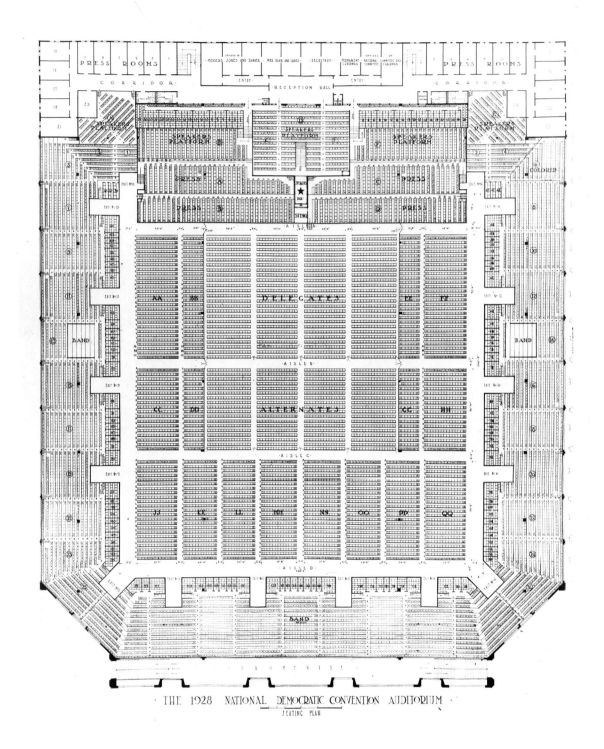

THE 1928 NATIONAL DEMOCRATIC CONVENTION AUDITORIUM
SEATING PLAN

Floor plan showing the seating arrangements for delegates, press, bands, and dignitaries attending the 1928 Democratic National Convention. The small, segregated area reserved for African Americans can be seen in the upper right-hand portion of the seating plan. (Democratic Convention Hall Vertical File, Courtesy HMRC, Houston Public Library.)

The Convention Hall can be seen in the far-right portion of this ca. 1928 photograph, giving some idea of the building's enormous size. The Esperson Building, the Federal Land Bank Building, and the Houston Public Library (now the Julia Ideson Building) are visible in the lower-left corner. Remarkably, all three buildings are still extant. (MSS 334-832, Courtesy HMRC, Houston Public Library.)

Fourth Ward/Freedmen's Town

No AREA OF HOUSTON deserves the title of "lost" more than Freedmen's Town, the African American community whose boundaries were contained within the city's Fourth Ward. Although the ward's boundaries were larger than the original area of Freedmen's Town, the two designations were often used interchangeably. While the center of African American commercial and residential activity later shifted to the Fifth and Third wards, Freedmen's Town remained synonymous with a thriving, well-established African American culture in the minds of many Houstonians. With its concentration of African American-owned businesses, nightclubs, theaters, and restaurants, Freedmen's Town was the closest thing to a Harlem-like environment that many Houstonians had ever experienced. The destruction of the vibrant social and cultural life of this community was brought about over the years by a series of development projects that were definitely not to the benefit of Fourth Ward residents. So few original buildings remain extant today in Freedmen's Town that it looks as if an atomic bomb had hit the area, requiring its total redevelopment.

Despite the atmosphere of community and self-identification that the Fourth Ward provided African Americans in an era of strict racial segregation, living conditions were by no means idyllic for all its residents. A 1929 report by the National Urban League noted that the streets and housing were often in poor condition and that city services were not being extended to black neighborhoods. In addition, the U.S. Supreme Court's "separate but equal" ruling in *Plessy v. Ferguson* resulted in public facilities that were separate, but rarely equal. Segregation cast a pall over Houston's African American community until the civil rights movement brought about change.

Houston College football players with campus buildings in the background, 1914. The segregated, blacks-only school located on San Felipe Road advertised itself as a "literary and industrial school." (MSS 100-855, Courtesy HMRC, Houston Public Library.)

Members of the Houston Negro Chamber of Commerce pose in front of the Chamber's office, located in the 400 block of Milam. African American businessmen and professionals such as these served as one of the strongest foundations of Houston's segregated black middle class. (MSS 190-125, Courtesy HMRC, Houston Public Library.)

This aerial shot of Jefferson Davis Hospital, taken near the time of the hospital's completion in 1937, inadvertently shows the pre–World War II character of the Fourth Ward to the south of the hospital grounds, with churches, businesses, and rows of shotgun houses. The clearance of homes to make way for the construction of the hospital was one of the first large-scale alterations to this historic area of Freedmen's Town. The wholesale destruction of the adjacent neighborhood initiated a trend that would last throughout the remainder of the twentieth century and continue into the twenty-first. (RG D5-1031, Courtesy HMRC, Houston Public Library.)

The Art Moderne-styled Rainbow Theatre, ca. 1940. Located at 909 West Dallas, the Rainbow Theatre was typical of the businesses that lined that street, making it an important commercial corridor for African American businesses in the Fourth Ward. The Rainbow Shop, which sold men's and women's clothing, was located to the left of the theater entrance at 905 West Dallas. The Rainbow Theatre remained open until 1959. (MSS 210, Courtesy HMRC, Houston Public Library.)

The interior of the Deluxe Bar B-Q restaurant at 407 West Dallas, another black-owned business that shared in the Fourth Ward's thriving commerce during the first half of the twentieth century. Many businesses like the Deluxe were later forced to move or close as downtown Houston pushed westward and the area made way for construction of new, white-owned businesses and parking lots. (MSS-210, Courtesy HMRC, Houston Public Library.)

Architectural rendering of the Ancient Order of Pilgrims headquarters. In 1926, architect Alfred Finn designed the executive office building for the Supreme Home of the Ancient Order of Pilgrims, San Felipe Street at Bagby Avenue. This impressive structure, which also contained rented office space for black-owned businesses, signified for many years the civic importance of the Fourth Ward to Houston's African American community. (MSS 19-1320, Courtesy HMRC, Houston Public Library.)

African American businessmen pose in front of the offices of Drs. Lyons and Ferrill, located at 400 Milam. Almost every profession and white-owned business had its African American twin in an era of strict segregationist practices. (MSS 182-79, Courtesy HMRC, Houston Public Library.)

Street scene, West Dallas Avenue, ca. 1930s. This image conveys some of the vibrancy of the Fourth Ward's main commercial corridor prior to its destruction. (MSS 157-770R, Courtesy HMRC, Houston Public Library.)

Colored Carnegie Library

IT IS IMPOSSIBLE to measure the educational, social, and cultural influence that the Colored Carnegie Library had on Houston's African American community during the fifty years that it was in operation. Designed by William Sidney Pittman, a prominent African American architect and the son-in-law of Booker T. Washington, the library was built with Carnegie Foundation funds and completed in 1912. In the "separate but equal" atmosphere of the times, the Colored Carnegie was built to serve the needs of African Americans at a time when they were not allowed access to whites-only library facilities. In addition to meeting the needs of students and adult library patrons, the library was a venue for countless civic and professional meetings and events. The Colored Carnegie was demolished in 1962 to make way for the Pierce Elevated section of Interstate Highway 45. The library's destruction came to symbolize the eventual eradication of the Fourth Ward, since the completion of the Pierce Elevated physically split the Fourth Ward in two, a blow from which it never recovered.

Dedication ceremonies for the Colored Carnegie Library, 1912. (RG A13-2140, Courtesy HMRC, Houston Public Library.)

Front elevation (Frederick Street entrance) of Colored Carnegie Library, ca. 1911, by architect William Sidney Pittman. (RG D26-5, Courtesy HMRC, Houston Public Library.)

Two young library patrons pose in front of the Colored Carnegie branch in 1923. (RG A13-2148, Courtesy HMRC, Houston Public Library.)

City officials and African American civic leaders inspect the cornerstone of the Colored Carnegie Library during its demolition in 1962. (RG A13-2144, Courtesy HMRC, Houston Public Library.)

— Theatre Row —

EW PLACES EVOKE greater nostalgia and sense of loss for Houston's past than a mere mention of the grand movie palaces that lined "Theatre Row" on Main Street. The three principal film palaces on Theatre Row were Loew's State Theatre, the Metropolitan Theatre, and the Majestic Theatre. There were also other less opulent popular theaters such as the Kirby along Theatre Row, but it is primarily the "big three" that Houstonians most remember. Prior to the advent of television, the opening of a blockbuster film like *Gone with the Wind*, which was shown at Loew's State, were community events. In the case of *Gone with the Wind*,

some schools even dismissed classes so that students would be able to see the movie during daylight hours (the film's length precluded most children from attending in the evening).

Because films were the entertainment of choice across Houston's ethnic and class lines, the theaters that constituted Theatre Row are remembered with an awe that sometimes borders on reverence. Not only did these theaters show the major studios' first-run releases, but they also transported patrons to another world with the grandiosity of their elaborate Egyptian and Classical revival interiors.

Houston's "Theatre Row" along Main Street, ca. 1920s. The marquees of the Metropolitan, Loew's State, and Kirby theaters are visible. (MSS 200-175, Courtesy HMRC, Houston Public Library.)

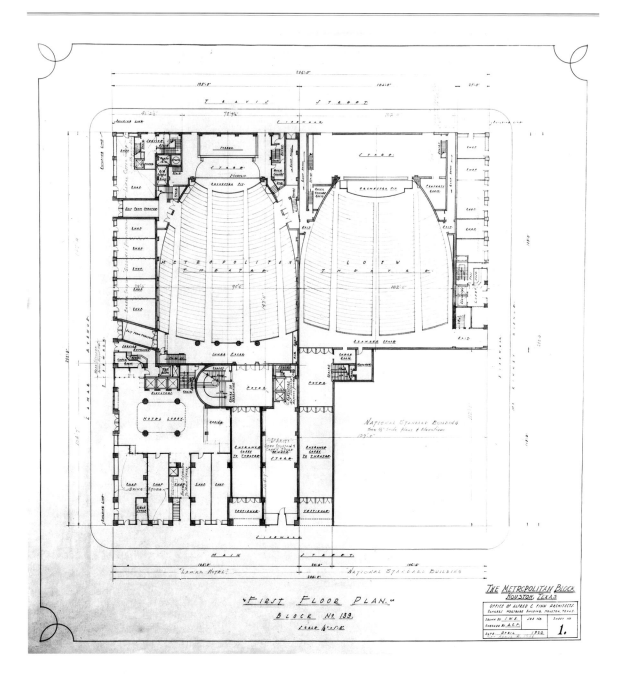

First floor plan of the Metropolitan Block by Alfred Finn, 1926, showing the first-floor layouts of both the Metropolitan and Loew's theaters. The Main Street entrances to the two theaters were virtually side-by-side. (MSS 19-Job 345, Courtesy HMRC, Houston Public Library.)

Loew's State Theatre

MANY HOUSTONIANS regarded Loew's State Theatre as the grandest and most prestigious of all the "Big Three" Main Street movie palaces. For forty years, it was the only theater that the Loew's chain constructed in Houston. In keeping with the nationwide, upscale image of Loew's theaters, the Houston Loew's was kept in immaculate condition and filled to the brim with antique vases, statuary, and furniture—although some claimed that the "antiques" were of dubious origin.

The interior of Loew's State, yet another Alfred Finn design, employed Classical motifs. Like the adjacent Metropolitan Theatre, Loew's façade was unimpressive, since it was sited within an innocuous-looking office building. As patrons entered the theater's lobby through highly polished bronze doors, however, they were greeted with an onslaught of decorative artwork. They were then funneled through a long corridor with a low-slung ceiling, which made stepping into the beautiful, spacious, elaborate auditorium a stunning experience.

Located at 1022 Main, the 2,519-seat Loew's opened in 1927 and remained operational as a movie theater until 1972, when it was demolished.

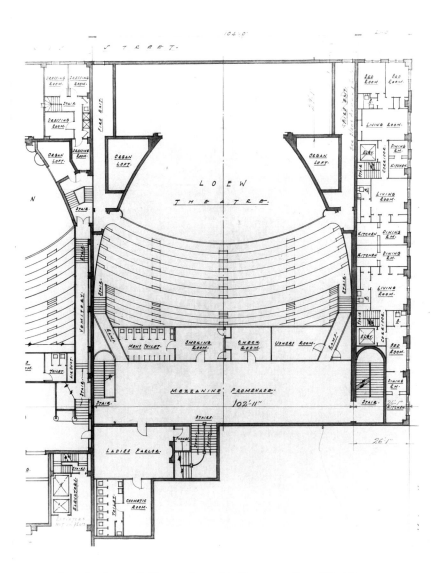

Floor plan for Loew's Theatre, designed by Houston architect Alfred Finn, 1925.
(MSS 19 Job 357, Courtesy HMRC, Houston Public Library.)

Loew's Theatre near completion, 1927. The neighboring Metropolitan Theatre can be seen on the left. (MSS 19-888, Courtesy HMRC, Houston Public Library.)

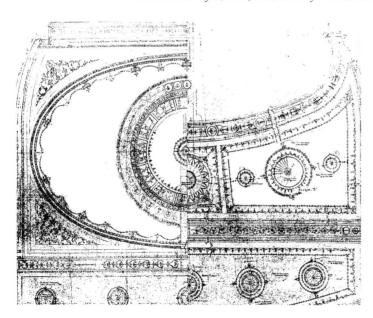

Detail of reflected ceiling plan for Loew's Theatre, 1926. (MSS 19 Job 357, Courtesy HMRC, Houston Public Library.)

Entrance lobby, as seen from theater auditorium, ca. 1928. Finn provided the same level of detailing for the Loew's entranceway that he gave to the theater's interior. The featured entertainer when this photo was taken was the popular bandleader Jan Garber, who was nicknamed "The Idol of the Air Lanes" after gaining fame on radio broadcasts. (MSS 19-390, Courtesy HMRC, Houston Public Library.)

West wall of Loew's auditorium, ca. 1927. This shot provides a better look at Loew's beautiful ornamentation, including numerous classical medallions, that decorated the walls of the theater and portions of its ceiling. (MSS 19-397, Courtesy HMRC, Houston Public Library.)

*Gentlemen's lounge, Loew's Theatre, ca. 1927.
(MSS 19-1462, Courtesy HMRC, Houston Public Library.)*

*Proscenium of Loew's Theatre, ca. 1927. Note the beautiful classical relief work
above the stage. (MSS 19-400, Courtesy HMRC, Houston Public Library.)*

Loew's balcony section and ornate ceiling, with its massive circular medallion and chandelier, ca. 1928. (MSS 19-398, Courtesy HMRC, Houston Public Library.)

Loew's entry lobby as seen in the late 1960s. Even though the theater was only a few years away from demolition, it was still maintained in good condition, complete with its highly polished bronze doors seen in the lower left of the photograph. (MSS 157-798, Courtesy HMRC, Houston Public Library.)

All that remained of the beautiful Loew's Theatre following its demolition in August 1973. An advertisement for the Metropolitan can still be seen on one of the remaining walls behind the piles of rubble and scrap metal. All of Houston's "big three" movie palaces suffered the same fate. (RG D6, Courtesy HMRC, Houston Public Library.)

Metropolitan Theatre

IN SPITE OF the fact that a newspaper critic once derided the Metropolitan Theatre as "an Egyptian nightmare," the Metropolitan was selected by *American Theaters of Today*, a 1930 survey of theaters, as one of the top theaters built in the United States during the late 1920s. The Metropolitan was most likely the only building in Houston that ever used the Egyptian revival style, although it was only used in the theater's interior. While the Metropolitan may have had the only Egyptian revival interior in town, its lack of stylemates was more than compensated for by the profusion of faux Egyptian decorative detail work that almost overpowered the first-time patron.

Like its neighbor, Loew's State, the Metropolitan was located in the Metropolitan Block, a Jesse H. Jones project, with its entrance on Main and its auditorium alongside Travis Street. Alfred Finn designed the Metropolitan and received detailing assistance from well-known theater architect John Eberson, who had earlier designed the Majestic Theatre. The Metropolitan seated 3,000 people and was equipped with a hydraulic orchestra pit that raised the orchestra from the pit to stage level at the close of each film, readying it for the stage show, which, until the Great Depression, always followed film presentations. Final construction costs amounted to two million dollars. The Metropolitan opened on Christmas Day 1926 with the silent film *Stranded in Paris* starring Bebe Daniels.

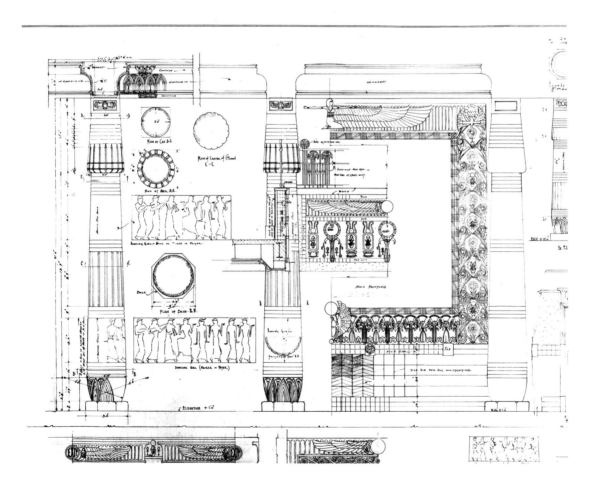

Drawing of ornamental section details by Alfred Finn, Metropolitan Theatre, 1925.
(MSS 19-Job 345, Courtesy HMRC, Houston Public Library.)

Interior view showing balcony and ceiling ornamentation, ca. 1927. (MSS 19-419, Courtesy HMRC, Houston Public Library.)

Highly ornate entrance hall of the Metropolitan, ca. 1927. (MSS 19-425, Courtesy HMRC, Houston Public Library.)

Proscenium arch of the Metropolitan Theatre as seen from the balcony, ca. 1927. The sacred Egyptian vulture deity, Nekhebet, is featured above the proscenium. The copious faux Egyptian ornamentation used to decorate the Metropolitan was both admired by many theater patrons and derided by others as 1920s excess at its worst. (MSS 19-410, Courtesy HMRC, Houston Public Library.)

Majestic Theatre

THE MAJESTIC THEATRE, completed in 1923 and located at 908 Rusk, was the first of the "big three" movie palaces to be built in the area of downtown Houston that would later be known as Theatre Row. Designed by famed Chicago theater architect John Eberson, the Majestic Theatre attracted national attention as the first in the United States to feature an atmospheric ceiling. The Majestic's ceiling featured hundreds of twinkling lights and drifting cloud formations to give the audience the feeling that they were outdoors at dusk or twilight. Atmospheric ceilings became very popular in American theater construction during the remainder of the 1920s. The Majestic's architectural style was primarily Italian Renaissance revival, but Greco-Roman decorative motifs were also employed in the design. The interior seating area was constructed to resemble an outdoor Italian garden and floral designs decorated the entry ceiling.

An avalanche of publicity preceded the Majestic's opening on January 29, 1923, with Dallas movie theater entrepreneur Karl Hoblitzell presiding over the opening ceremonies. In addition to showing films, the Majestic presented live vaudeville and stage shows. During the Majestic's early years, the silent films were practically a sideline entertainment in comparison to the popularity of the live shows.

By 1970, like many other notable American film venues, the Majestic was showing X-rated films. In April 1971, the Majestic's site was sold for $1.4 million. The theater closed its doors on September 26 that same year and was demolished a short time later. Even though architectural drawings for some of Eberson's numerous other theaters still survive—most notably the plans for his atmospheric Majestic Theatre in San Antonio—no drawings have ever been located for Houston's Majestic. In addition, fewer photos have survived of Houston's Majestic compared to the documentation that exists for so many other Houston movie houses, possibly because it was the earliest of the city's major movie theaters.

Interior view from the balcony of John Eberson's beautiful Majestic Theatre.
(Litterst-Dixon Collection, Courtesy HMRC, Houston Public Library.)

Exterior of Kirby Theatre, another Theatre Row venue, ca. 1932. Grand Hotel *won the Academy Award for Best Picture of 1932, and the theater's promotion for the film included a fake hotel marquee. (*MSS 200-129, Courtesy HMRC, Houston Public Library.*)*

The Iris Theatre, at 614 Travis, was part of the Publix chain of theaters. This photo was taken in December 1929 following a rare Houston snowstorm on December 22 (the slush is still visible along the curb), which dropped 2.5 inches of snow. Christmas lights are strung along the arcade, and Christmas trees, presumably for sale, can be seen in the lower left-hand portion of the photo. Released more than two years after The Jazz Singer, *the featured Hoot Gibson comedy,* Courtin' Wildcats, *was still being promoted as a "talkie." (Iris Theatre Vertical File, Courtesy* HMRC, *Houston Public Library.)*

Zoe Theatre

Houston had other downtown theaters besides the prestigious movie palaces of Theatre Row. The Zoe Theatre was located at 719 Main. Architect Alfred Finn's office, which he maintained at this location during 1919–1920, can be seen in the upper-left portion of the photo, above the Zoe's entrance arcade. This shot was taken ca. 1920, when the theater's feature film was The U.P. Trail, a Zane Grey Western. (MSS 19-1418, Courtesy HMRC, Houston Public Library.)

— Village Theatre —

THE VILLAGE THEATRE, designed by the noted firm of MacKie & Kamrath for the Interstate Theatres chain, was typical of the many neighborhood theaters that multiplied outside Houston's downtown core once suburbanization began in earnest during the 1930s. MacKie & Kamrath won national recognition for their modernist design when the 960-seat theater opened in 1941, the last Houston theater to be completed before the outbreak of World War II. As late as the 1970s, the Village was still showing first-run films like *Barry Lyndon* and *The Exorcist*, but it later deteriorated to showing only X-rated movies. Rice University, the theater's owner, demolished the Village in January 1994 after film buffs and preservationists had made several attempts to save the building. Today only a reconstructed version of the theater's marquee marks the spot where the Village once stood.

The Village Theatre in 1950. The theater's marquee was a neighborhood landmark. (Courtesy Bob Bailey Studios Photographic Archive, The Center for American History, The University of Texas at Austin.)

Interior shot of the Village Theatre, taken from the balcony, ca. 1941. Note the sleek, sparse design of the interior, which contrasted greatly with the opulence of downtown theaters such as Loew's or the Metropolitan. (Courtesy Bob Bailey Studios Photographic Archive, The Center for American History, The University of Texas at Austin.)

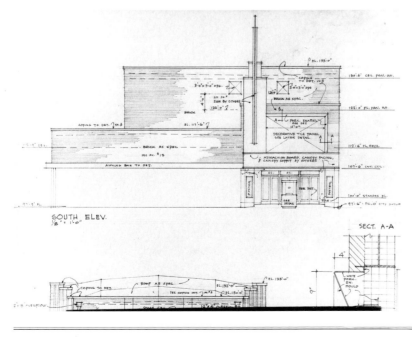

South elevation of the Village Theatre by MacKie & Kamrath, 1940. (MacKie & Kamrath Collection, Job 41-503, Courtesy HMRC, Houston Public Library.)

— Granada Theater —

Granada Theater, 1949. The Spanish/tropical-themed Granada, located at 9231 Jensen near Tidwell, was a favorite entertainment venue for Houstonians from the city's near-northeast neighborhoods for many years prior to its closing. The Granada opened on December 7, 1949. (MSS 200-113, Courtesy HMRC, Houston Public Library.)

*Interior of the Granada Theater, ca. 1949. The wall murals portrayed an amalgam of flamingos, coy
senoritas, and guitar-strumming, serenading, romantic Spanish men, and the carpets were woven with
Moorish motifs. (MSS 200-118, Courtesy HMRC, Houston Public Library.)*

— Camp Logan —

Only the smallest physical traces remains today of the U.S. Army's Camp Logan, a "city" of over 20,000 residents that was constructed in 1917 on land that was then located at the western edge of Houston where Memorial Park is now located. Despite its economic and historic importance (it became infamous because of a race riot involving soldiers from the camp), the only remnants of Camp Logan are a few scattered place names, one original building on Washington Avenue, and scattered chunks of concrete in Memorial Park.

In 1917, the Army acquired approximately 2,000 acres along Buffalo Bayou, following a hard-fought lobbying effort by the City to have the training base situated in Houston. Within a matter of weeks after the initial construction began, on July 24, more than 1,000 buildings had been constructed, and more than 20,000 soldiers (some estimates state as high as 30,000) were assigned to the camp by World War I's end in November 1918. Camp Logan was virtually a self-contained city. In ad-

dition to barracks, roads, and bridges, Camp Logan had its own library, movie theater, hospital, and other necessary facilities and amenities for the troops. Olle Lorehn, at the time one of Houston's most prolific architects, is believed to have designed some of the buildings in the camp, including the theater.

With the close of the war and the demobilization of troops, Camp Logan was soon leveled. About 1,000 acres of the land on which it was constructed was later bought by the City from Will and Mike Hogg and dedicated as Memorial Park (in honor of American troops who had served during World War I) in 1924. In the wooded areas of the park, occasional pieces of concrete from the construction of Camp Logan can still be found.

Apart from these pieces, no discerning visitor to Memorial Park would know that a mini-city had once existed there for several years. The following scenes of Camp Logan were all originally issued as postcards for purchase by the troops.

(Censored) Main Street, Showing Mess Halls—Camp Logan, Houston, Texas.

Camp Logan's unpaved and muddy Main Street, ca. 1917–1918. (MSS 187-006, Courtesy HMRC, Houston Public Library.)

(Censored)   Infirmary—Camp Logan, Houston, Texas.

Prior to its release for use on a postcard, this photo of Camp Logan's large infirmary ca. 1917–1918 was censored for wartime security reasons. (MSS 187-012, Courtesy HMRC, Houston Public Library.)

2107—REGIMENTAL STREET—
CAMP LOGAN, TEXAS

Regimental Street showing the barracks that were quickly constructed to house the troops in 1917. (MSS 187-024, Courtesy HMRC, Houston Public Library.)

The Young Men's Christian Association (Y.M.C.A.) established an on-site presence at Camp Logan to provide wholesome activities for the soldiers. (MSS 187-029, Courtesy HMRC, Houston Public Library.)

Camp Logan's library was established in 1917 with the cooperation of the American Library Association. (MSS 187-036, Courtesy HMRC, Houston Public Library.)

Architect Olle Lorehn is credited with having designed some of Camp Logan's structures. The Liberty Theatre (1917), located within the grounds of Camp Logan, is sometimes attributed to Lorehn, but Alfred Finn actually designed the theater for the Majestic Circuit. A set of drawings for the theater is located in the Alfred Finn architectural collection. (MSS 114-600, Courtesy HMRC, Houston Public Library.)

— South End Christian Church —

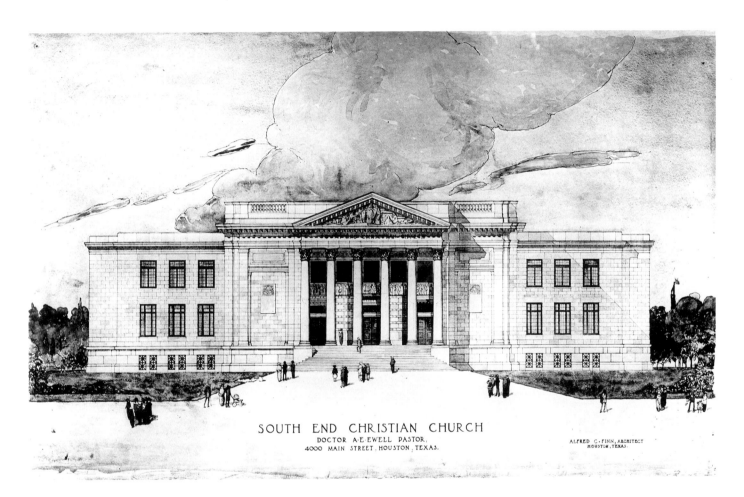

SOUTH END CHRISTIAN CHURCH
DOCTOR A·E·EWELL PASTOR,
4000 MAIN STREET, HOUSTON, TEXAS.

ALFRED C·FINN, ARCHITECT
HOUSTON, TEXAS.

Rendering of the South End Christian Church designed in 1922 by Alfred Finn. The imposing neoclassical edifice stood at 4000 Main Street and was constructed at a time when the South End was populated by many of Houston's more affluent citizens. (MSS 19-1311, Courtesy HMRC, Houston Public Library.)

— Captain John's Sea Foods Restaurant —

Captain John's Sea Food Restaurant, located at 1927 West Gray, was a favorite eating place of Houstonians for decades. This photo, taken in the late 1970s, provides a good view of the restaurant's nautically themed, Art Moderne architecture. The site is currently occupied by a Pier 1 Imports Store. (MSS 97-58, Courtesy HMRC, Houston Public Library.)

— Miller Memorial Theater —

The classically elegant Miller Memorial Theater, located in Hermann Park, was designed by William Ward Watkin in 1921. The theater was demolished beginning in 1967 to make way for the present Miller Outdoor Theater, completed in 1969. The only remnants of Watkin's original theater are the columns, which flanked both sides of the proscenium. The columns were moved in 1968 to help create the Mecom-Rockwell Fountain and Colonnade at the north end of Hermann Park near the ZaZa Hotel (formerly the Warwick Hotel). (MSS 157-796, Courtesy HMRC, Houston Public Library.)

— Contemporary Arts Museum —

Rendering of the Contemporary Arts Museum (CAM), ca. 1948, by the firm of MacKie & Kamrath. This simple, but modernistic A-frame structure was designed as the first gallery and exhibition space for Houston's Contemporary Arts Association, founded in 1948. Eventually, this building, located at 502 Dallas, became too small for the needs of the CAM, and it moved to its present, more spacious location on the northwest corner of Montrose and Bissonnet in 1972. Famed author Donald Barthelme served for a period of time as the museum's acting director. (MacKie & Kamrath Collection, Job 48-115, Courtesy HMRC, Houston Public Library.)

— Pepsi-Cola Bottling Plant —

The Pepsi-Cola Bottling Plant was located at 6626 Gulf Freeway. Its trademark Saarinen-like arch and Modernist design made the building stand apart from other industrial and manufacturing sites along the freeway. The plant is memorable to baby boomers for another reason as well. During the 1950s–1960s, the arch was outlined with Christmas lights each holiday season and enormous wrapped packages were placed at its base to give the arch the appearance of a giant Christmas tree. (MSS 243-540, Courtesy HMRC, Houston Public Library.)

— Best Products Showroom —

In Houston, even buildings as stylistically new as the Best Products Store are demolished and gone without a trace in a matter of only a few years. Best Products' surprising exterior was a favorite (or a bane, depending on perspective) of many Houstonians during its short life. Located on Kleckley Street near the Almeda-Genoa Mall, the Houston store was the first of several "Indeterminate Facades" built around the country. The Best Products Showroom was purposely designed and built as a ruin, with a cascade of bricks tumbling down its front exterior. The idea came from a group of New York City-based conceptual artists whose architectural work would later be labeled "deconstructivist." Despite the fact that the building initially drew large numbers of customers, by the 1990s lagging business prompted the placing of neon lights around the exterior, and the showroom was demolished a few years later. (MSS 19-13, Courtesy H M R C, Houston Public Library.)

—— Jefferson Davis Hospital ——

THE JEFFERSON DAVIS Hospital was designed by the two most prominent Houston architects of the 1930s, Alfred C. Finn and Joseph Finger, in the Moderne style. The cornerstone was laid on July 8, 1936. During its construction phase, the hospital was known as simply City-County Hospital to distinguish it from its immediate predecessor, which was also named Jefferson Davis Hospital and was still in operation pending completion of City-County. The central tower of the hospital was eleven stories high, while the two adjoining wings were ten stories. Dedicated in October 1937, a mere fifteen months after beginning construction, the 500-bed Jefferson Davis Hospital was itself replaced in 1989 by the Lyndon B. Johnson Hospital located in Houston's near-north side. Despite ardent pleas by preservationists and the floating of numerous alternative uses for the empty structure, the building was demolished in 1999 and Houston lost one of its finest remaining Moderne structures. Today, the Houston branch of the Federal Reserve Bank occupies the site. Ironically, the first Jefferson Davis Hospital, at Elder and Girard Streets, still stands, only partially as a result of its historic value. The hospital grounds contained numerous graves of Civil War veterans, both Confederate and Union, and civilians, both African American and white, causing the halt of demolition efforts. It was a case of a fairly frequent mode of historic preservation—the halting of demolition as a result of unforeseen, inadvertent circumstances.

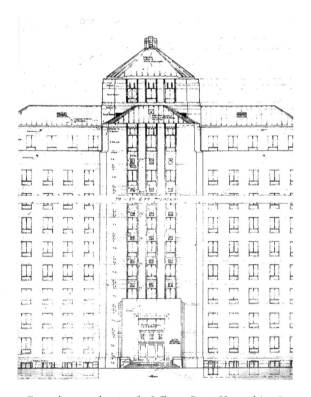

Front elevation drawing for Jefferson Davis Hospital (1936), which was known during its construction phase as simply the "City-County Hospital." (MSS 19-Job 421, Courtesy HMRC, Houston Public Library.)

Jefferson Davis Hospital, shortly after its completion in 1937. (MSS 19-825, Courtesy HMRC, Houston Public Library.)

Aerial perspective rendering showing Alfred Finn's proposal for an expansion of the Jefferson Davis Hospital in the 1950s. (MSS 19-748, Courtesy HMRC, Houston Public Library.)

St. Paul's Methodist Church

This classically elegant, Grecian-styled building opened in 1909 and was the home to the St. Paul's Methodist Church congregation prior to moving to its current location on South Main in 1930. St. Paul's was crowned with a distinctive Byzantine dome. In less than two decades the growth of St. Paul's congregation necessitated both the purchase of a new site and construction of a new sanctuary. (MSS 187-296, Courtesy HMRC, Houston Public Library.)

Oak Farms Dairy Company

Originally constructed as the Carnation Dairy and later, the home of the Oak Farms Dairy, this Art Moderne building stood as a landmark at 701 Waugh for many years. Designed by Moderne specialist Joseph Finger, the dairy was completed in 1947. In the early decades of the twentieth century, Houston had several dairies located within or adjacent to the city limits, another indication of how rural much of the Houston area was at that time. (MSS 97-68, Courtesy HMRC, Houston Public Library.)

A closer view of the dairy's streamlined Moderne architecture. Architect Joseph Finger was nearing the end of his stellar career when the Carnation Dairy was completed, but the reasons for his prominence as Houston's outstanding modernistic architect during the 1920s–1930s were still evident just six years before his death. (MSS 97-53, Courtesy HMRC, Houston Public Library.)

——— Sam Houston Coliseum and Music Hall ———

THE SAM HOUSTON Music Hall and Coliseum comprised part of Houston's new Art Deco Civic Center when it was completed in 1937. The complex was one of the many Public Works Administration (PWA) projects that Jesse H. Jones, in his role as head of the Reconstruction Finance Corporation, helped to fund in Houston. Alfred Finn, Jones' favored "in-house" architect, utilized the Moderne style when designing the Music Hall and Coliseum and employed abstract, zigzag motifs in his detailing work. The total costs amounted to some $1,300,00.

Prior to the completion of Jones Hall in 1967, eminent conductors such as Leopold Stokowski, Sir John Barborolli, and Andre Previn led the Houston Symphony Orchestra in performances at the Music Hall. The Music Hall also played host to traveling Broadway musicals, and, on August 19, 1965, the Beatles made their only Houston appearance on the Music Hall stage. In addition, wrestling matches broadcast from the Coliseum were a staple of early Houston television programming.

The Coliseum was home to the Houston Fat Stock Show and Livestock Exposition (changed to Houston Livestock Show and Rodeo in 1961) prior to the construction of the Astrodome. In 1938, only a year after the completion of the Coliseum, Finn designed a one-story addition on the building's north side for use as a cattle barn during livestock exhibitions. This addition was also used to house circus menageries when circuses played the Coliseum. In 1955, the entire complex was enlarged and air conditioned by the firm of Lloyd and Morgan. Both the Music Hall and Coliseum were demolished in 1998 to make way for the construction of the Hobby Center for the Performing Arts.

EXPOSITION AND CONVENTION HALL
HOUSTON ⚬ TEXAS

Early rendering of the Sam Houston Coliseum and Music Hall completed in Alfred Finn's office, 1936. (MSS 19-Job 444A, Courtesy HMRC, Houston Public Library.)

EXPOSITION and CONVENTION HALL
HOUSTON TEXAS

ALFRED C. FINN-ARCHITECT
HOUSTON TEXAS
ROBERT J. CUMMINS-CONSULTING ENGINEER

The refined presentation rendering of the Sam Houston Coliseum prepared by Alfred Finn's office, 1936. The Coliseum is labeled as the "Exposition and Convention Hall." (MSS 19-736, Courtesy HMRC, Houston Public Library.)

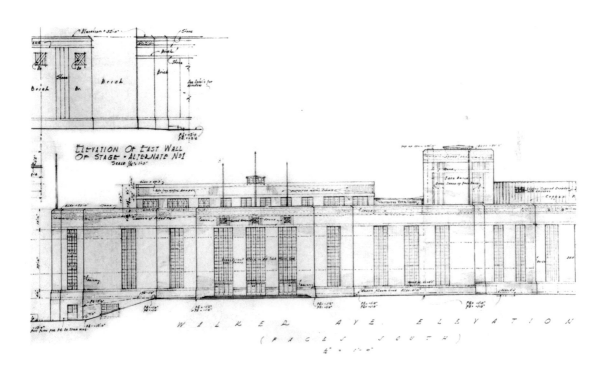

ELEVATION OF EAST WALL
OF STAGE - ALTERNATE N°1

WALKER AVE. ELEVATION
(FACES SOUTH)

The Walker Avenue elevation drawing of the Coliseum providing a southward view of the facility, 1936. (MSS 19-Job 444A, Courtesy HMRC, Houston Public Library.)

View of the Music Hall's interior seen from the balcony looking toward the stage, 1937. (MSS 19-737, Courtesy HMRC, Houston Public Library.)

View of the Music Hall's interior seen from the stage, 1937. (MSS 19-738, Courtesy HMRC, Houston Public Library.)

The newly completed Sam Houston Coliseum and Music Hall, 1937. The photo was taken from a window of Houston's new City Hall, still under construction. (MSS 19-733, Courtesy HMRC, Houston Public Library.)

— Humble Oil and Refining Company Filling Station #4 —

Humble Oil and Refining Company Filling Station #4 was completed in 1919 and stood on the corner of Main and Jefferson. This station was likely considered a prototype for future Humble Oil service stations, as the company employed Alfred Finn to design the station rather than relying on an in-house architect or engineer. Humble Oil was not anxious to join the burgeoning ranks of retail gasoline distributors, but the company had recently acquired the Dixie refinery, an operator of curbside pumps. Gulf Oil had constructed the first service station only six years before in Pittsburgh. The lavish Filling Station #4 was built at a cost of $50,000, and the interior, decorated with mosaic tiles, contained cases displaying auto-related goods for sale. The photo shows the station shortly after its completion. (MSS 19-813, Courtesy HMRC, Houston Public Library. Historical information from Humble Oil Filling Station Vertical File.)

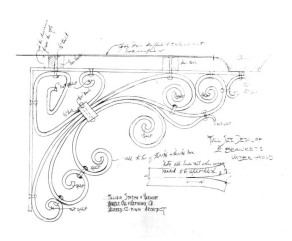

Detail of brackets used to support the portico hood of Filling Station #4, 1918. Architectural drawing by Alfred Finn's office. (MSS 19-Job 168, Courtesy HMRC, Houston Public Library.)

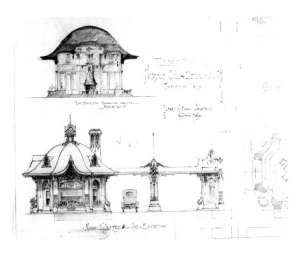

Elevation drawing of Filling Station #4, designed by Alfred Finn, 1918. The drawing was executed with watercolors. (MSS 19-Job 168, Courtesy HMRC, Houston Public Library.)

Almost every city and town of any size or importance in the United States in the first half of the twentieth century had a Woolworth's department store. Houston's downtown branch was located at 920 Main Street. The photo can be dated to 1917–1918, because during that time architect Alfred Finn maintained an office, visible on the left side of the second floor, in the Woolworth Building. When Woolworth store chain founder Frank W. Woolworth died in 1919, there were over one thousand Woolworth stores in the United States alone. (MSS 19-1317, *Courtesy* HMRC, *Houston Public Library.*)

Houston Post Building

Main entrance, Houston Post Building. The Houston Post Building had beautiful ornamentation and detailing on its exterior. "The Post" was spelled out with electric light bulbs at the top of the building, still something of a novelty when the building was completed in 1902. Designed by Chicago Prairie School architect Carbys Zimmerman, the Houston Post Building served as the newspaper's headquarters. The local supervising architect was Swedish-born transplant Olle Lorehn, who moved to Houston from St. Louis in 1893. Lorehn also designed Houston's first "skyscraper," the six-story Binz Building. (MSS 145-156, Courtesy HMRC, Houston Public Library.)

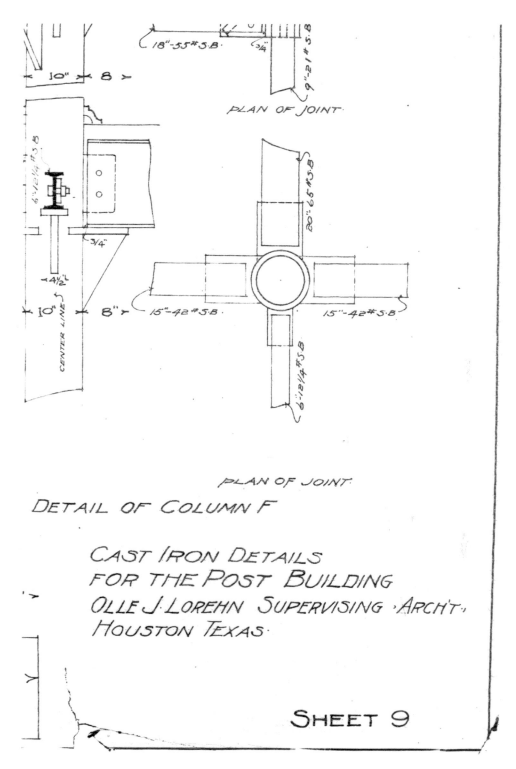

PLAN OF JOINT

PLAN OF JOINT.

DETAIL OF COLUMN F

CAST IRON DETAILS
FOR THE POST BUILDING
OLLE J. LOREHN SUPERVISING · ARCH'T·
HOUSTON TEXAS·

SHEET 9

Detail of cast-iron work for a column for the Post building, 1902. This architectural drawing is fairly rare, as few drawings of architect Olle Lorehn's work still survive, despite the fact that he was one of the city's most prominent architects during the early twentieth century. (Olle Lorehn Collection, Houston Post Building, Sheet 9, Courtesy HMRC, Houston Public Library.)

— Metropole Hotel —

This is the only known interior photograph of the Metropole Hotel, ca. 1925, and it survives today only because the image was printed and distributed as a postcard. The Metropole was another Houston building designed by Swedish American architect Olle Lorehn. The hotel was never commissioned to be a design masterpiece, but was intended to provide easy access for train passengers wanting to stay near Union Station. The hotel was located at the corner of Preston and Crawford, only one block north of the train station. The Metropole was demolished in 1998 as part of the clearance process to make way for the Minute Maid Park and its surrounding parking lots. (MSS 145-128, Courtesy HMRC, Houston Public Library.)

—— Houston Fire Alarm Building ——

THE FIRE ALARM BUILDING, located on the northwest corner of Bagby and Lamar, was significant because it was the first Modernist structure authorized in Houston for municipal use, and its commissioning by the City of Houston meant that Modernism had arrived as an accepted style. The designers, Fred MacKie and Karl Kamrath, were among the first proponents of Modernism to practice architecture in Houston. Completed in 1939, the two-story rectangular building served as the central location for the city's fire alarm systems and also contained offices. Intended to be part of Houston's Civic Center, the Fire Alarm Building was intended to be compatible with Joseph Finger's new Moderne City Hall, which was also under construction at the time.

Completed at a cost of $60,000, the building was quickly embraced by Houstonians, despite the scarcity of local modernistic structures. In 1939, *Architectural Record* magazine conducted a poll to determine the most popular recently constructed buildings in Houston. The Fire Alarm Building surprisingly took second place in the survey. Within only a few decades, the population growth of Houston, coupled with rapid advances in technology, rendered the building obsolete. Dispatchers moved to a new location in 1975, and the building was used only occasionally for storage until it was destroyed in the 1980s. The site is now part of Sam Houston Park.

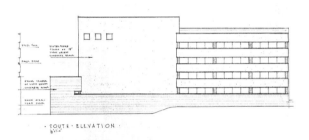

South elevation drawing of the Houston Fire Alarm Building, designed by MacKie & Kamrath, 1938. (Hare & Hare Collection, RG D26-3, Courtesy HMRC, Houston Public Library.)

Front elevation drawing (1938) of the Houston Fire Alarm Building, completed in 1939. The noted Kansas City landscaping firm of Hare and Hare, which designed numerous city parks in Houston over the course of several decades, was responsible for the layout of the building's grounds. (Hare & Hare Collection, RG D26-3, Courtesy HMRC, Houston Public Library.)

—— Houston Press Building ——

The newly completed headquarters of the Houston Press *newspaper, January 1928. Designed by the Cleveland, Ohio-based firm of Howell & Rusk, the Italianate-style building, on the corner of Rusk and Chartres, was formally opened on the following St. Valentine's Day, and the public was offered tours of the new facility. The* Press *(no relation to the current* Houston Press*) was owned by the Scripps-Howard chain and was one of Houston's three major daily newspapers until the* Chronicle *bought it out in 1964. (MSS 157-1105, Courtesy HMRC, Houston Public Library.)*

Houston City Hall and Market House (1904)

DESPITE THE FACT that the Victorian era officially came to a close with the death of Queen Victoria in 1901, its stylistic influences lingered on for years. Architect George Dickey designed Houston's fourth City Hall, completed in 1904, as an imposing, Victorian Romanesque structure. This building would serve as the city's seat of government for the next thirty-five years until the present City Hall was completed in 1939. Dickey's City Hall left a strong imprint on the city's civic consciousness as parades marched in front of the impressive structure, and many public events and ceremonies were held there.

In addition, the building left an impression on Houstonians for a more mundane reason: it was also the site of the Market House, where thousands of people shopped for fruits, vegetables, fish, and meat for many years. A new Market House was opened on Louisiana Street in 1929, and most first-floor tenants moved to the new market. The onset of the Great Depression that same year meant that the empty market stalls remained largely vacant throughout the 1930s.

City Hall lost both of its imposing towers in 1948 after inspections revealed serious structural defects. Following the move of city government in 1939 to the current City Hall, the "old" City Hall and Market House were eventually turned into a bus station. Much of the City Hall and Market House were destroyed by a five-alarm fire in 1960, and the remainder was finally demolished in 1962.

Texas A&M cadets march in procession past Houston's recently constructed City Hall in November 1909, prior to a football game. Houston's largest civic structure, the City Hall witnessed numerous parades, demonstrations, and other public events over the years. This photograph shows the Victorian structure's massive scale. (MSS 157-1062, Courtesy HMRC, Houston Public Library.)

Scenes at the City Market

Houston's Municipal Store established to regulate prices of other stall owners in city market

Vegetable and fruit stands inside of city market

Another interior view of city market.

Houston's curb market where farm products are sold by the farmer direct to the consumer.

These scenes of the City Hall Market were featured in the 1925 edition of the City Book of Houston. *Fresh produce from surrounding-area farms could be purchased at both interior shops and stalls, or alongside the street curb, where customers bought directly from local farmers. Locally caught fish were also sold in the interior fish market, which created odiferous conditions for city workers on hot, humid days. (From* City Book of Houston, *1925, p. 72, Courtesy* HMRC, *Houston Public Library.)*

Front elevation of the central part of the City Hall and Market House, by George Dickey, ca. 1903. The original drawing, executed on linen, imparts something of the structure's Victorian Romanesque grandeur, a style already outdated at the time of the building's completion. The building's interior was reportedly overstuffed with decorations and was soon too crowded for municipal employees. In style, the building's interior followed Sinclair Lewis's two-part definition of Victorian furnishings: First, every item must resemble something else from another period or style, and second, every inch of the interior must be filled with useless objects. (George Dickey Collection, 1034C-15, Courtesy HMRC, Houston Public Library.)

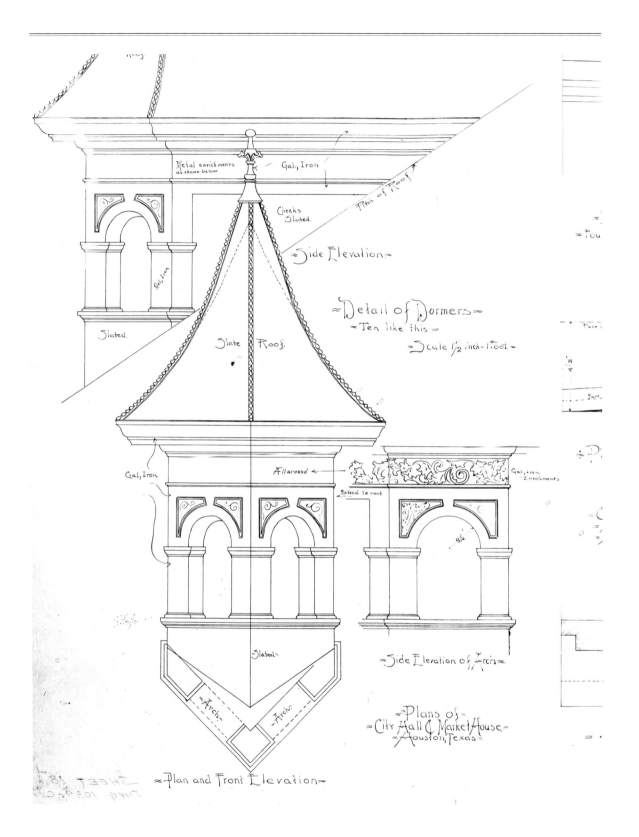

Metal enrichments
as shewn below.

Gal. Iron

Pitch of Roof

Cheeks
Slated.

= Side Elevation =

= Detail of Dormers =
= Ten like this =
= Scale 1½ inch = Foot =

Slate Roof.

Slated.

Gal. Iron

Gal. Iron

All around ←

Gal. Iron
Enrichments

Extend to roof

9½

Slated.

= Side Elevation of Arch =

Arch
Arch

= Plans of =
= City Hall & Market House, =
= Houston, Texas =

= Plan and Front Elevation =

Detail of dormers, front plan and elevation, City Hall and Market House, ca. 1903. Ten such dormers crowned the City Hall's roof. (George Dickey Collection, 1034C-18, Courtesy HMRC, Houston Public Library.)

Exterior view of the 1904 City Hall, showing produce delivery wagons parked outside. (MSS 157-994, Courtesy HMRC, Houston Public Library.)

The growth of municipal services and accompanying bureaucracy necessitated the building of an annex to the City Hall by the 1920s. (MSS 200-382, Courtesy HMRC, Houston Public Library.)

A photographer captured the City Hall's east tower as it collapsed during its demolition in 1948. Structural problems led to the demolition of both towers that year. When the remainder of the building was finally demolished in 1962, the outdated architecture, combined with the building's generally run-down appearance, was considered an eyesore by most Houstonians at the time, an outmoded reminder of a bygone era. (MSS 157-218R, Courtesy HMRC, Houston Public Library.)

Luna Park

In Houston, even amusement parks were tied to new technologies and the future. Luna Park, which opened in 1924, was widely advertised by its developers as "the Coney Island of Texas," named after a similar New York amusement park. The pre-opening publicity for the thirty-six-acre park, with the main entrance located in the 2200 block of Houston Street, stressed that Luna Park would feature all the latest technology in its attractions. One reporter went so far as to claim that the park's creators "gazed into the future" for inspiration when creating Luna Park's attractions. Although Houstonians responded enthusiastically to the new park and its many attractions, the onset of the Great Depression in 1929 sealed the park's fate. A portion of Interstate 10 now runs over part of the site where Luna Park once stood. (MSS 1248-2988, Courtesy HMRC, Houston Public Library.)

Foley Brothers Store

The exterior of Foley Brothers Department Store. Purchased by George and Robert Cohen of Galveston in 1919, Foley Brothers was already Houston's largest department store by the 1920s. The second incarnation of Foley Brothers Department store, Foley Brothers, was located in the 400 block of Main Street and opened in 1908. Foley Brothers was sold to Federated Department Stores in 1944 and subsequently moved again when a new, Kenneth Franzheim-designed store was completed at 1111 Main in 1947. (MSS 200-356, Courtesy HMRC, Houston Public Library.)

Foley Brothers devoted this show window to the patriotic cause of war bond purchases during World War II. (MSS 334-37, Courtesy HMRC, Houston Public Library.)

— Shamrock Hotel —

THE OPENING OF the Shamrock Hotel on March 17, 1949, might be the single most mythic moment in Houston's history. Built by oilman entrepreneur and wildcatter Glen McCarthy at a then staggering cost of $21 million, the 18-story, 1,001-room hotel's elaborate opening, complete with a parade down Main Street and a bevy of Hollywood stars, generated enormous hype and brought genuine nationwide attention to Houston for possibly the first time since the city hosted the Democratic National Convention in 1928. Only the opening of Foley's Department Store in 1947 had generated even remotely the coverage received by the Shamrock. Millions of Americans listened to the opening festivities, which were broadcast live by radio. In addition to omnipres-

ent radio and press coverage, the Shamrock's opening ceremonies were further imbedded in the American imagination when Edna Ferber's best-selling 1952 novel *Giant* was made into a film. Although the hotel in Ferber's novel was the Conquistador, the film portrays the opening of a fictionalized Shamrock Hotel, presided over by Jett Rink, a thinly disguised Glen McCarthy-type character.

Architect Wyatt C. Hedrick designed the Shamrock in what was virtually a last-gasp homage to the Moderne style, which was fading in popularity. While the hotel's exterior was relatively dull, the interior was a tribute to postwar American excess that has seldom been equaled. In recognition of McCarthy's Irish roots

Ground-level view of the Shamrock's exterior shortly after the hotel opened in March 1949.
(Uncataloged photo, Shamrock Hotel Vertical File, Courtesy HMRC, Houston Public Library.)

(aside from the obvious link to the name of the hotel and its debut on St. Patrick's Day), interior decorator Robert Harrell utilized sixty-three different shades of green throughout the hotel and dishware, wastebaskets, ashtrays, and other accessories were emblazoned with shamrocks or other Irish emblems. The Houston firm of Brochstein's Inc. was responsible for the hotel's beautiful interior design work, and Ralph Ellis Gunn served as the landscape architect for the lush grounds. When Frank Lloyd Wright visited Houston shortly after the opening of the hotel, architect Karl Kamrath took him to the Shamrock for an inspection. Wright is credited with two sarcastic quips regarding his visit. One was a simple question—"Why?"—and the other an observation: "I've always wanted to know what the inside of a jukebox looks like, and now I know."[1]

The ABC Radio Network broadcast a live music program from the Shamrock for several years titled "Saturday at the Shamrock." In its early years, the hotel was definitely a trendy place for celebrities to stay; some of the film stars who were guests included Dorothy Lamour, Bob Hope, Gene Autry, Bing Crosby, and Gene Tierney. By 1955, Glenn McCarthy's luck with oil discoveries had played out, and he sold his beloved Shamrock to the Hilton Hotels Corporation. It remained the Shamrock Hilton until 1985, when it was purchased by the Texas Medical Center. Despite spirited protests from thousands of preservationists, people from surrounding neighborhoods, history buffs, and other Houstonians—including Glen McCarthy himself—the Shamrock was demolished on June 1, 1987.

The Shamrock's famous Emerald Room, ca. 1949. The Emerald Room seated one thousand guests with enough room remaining for an orchestra and a large dance floor. (Brochstein's Inc. Shamrock Hotel Presentation Book, Shamrock Hotel Vertical File, Courtesy HMRC, Houston Public Library.)

A variety of high-end shops were located on the Shamrock's first floor for the convenience of hotel guests, including a women's clothing store, travel agency, drugstore, western wear shop, florist, barber shop, hairstyling salon, jewelry store and several other shops, including a branch of Sakowitz Brothers Department Store. (Brochstein's Inc. Shamrock Hotel Presentation Book, Shamrock Hotel Vertical File, Courtesy HMRC, *Houston Public Library.)*

The hotel's huge barbershop, ca. 1949. The barbershop featured an elegant, leather-upholstered settee for waiting customers. Even something as ordinary as a haircut was a luxurious experience at the Shamrock. (Brochstein's Inc. Shamrock Hotel Presentation Book, Shamrock Hotel Vertical File, Courtesy HMRC, Houston Public Library.)

The entrance to the bank of elevators off the Shamrock's main lobby was crowned with a stylized Art Moderne relief signifying the harnessing of energy. A suitably imposing portrait of hotel owner Glen McCarthy immodestly graced the opposite wall. (Brochstein's Inc. Shamrock Hotel Presentation Book, Shamrock Hotel Vertical File, Courtesy HMRC, Houston Public Library.)

The Shamrock Hotel's Cork Club, ca. 1949, was a well-known gathering spot for Houston's "Big Rich" for many years. An overabundance of shamrocks adorned the walls and furnishings, decorated in multiple shades of green. (Brochstein's Inc. Shamrock Hotel Presentation Book, Shamrock Hotel Vertical File, Courtesy HMRC, Houston Public Library.)

Glen McCarthy (third from left) poses with other Shamrock guests, including cowboy star Gene Autry (third from right). Autry was just one of scores of Hollywood celebrities who flocked to the Shamrock in its early years. Houston retail merchant and philanthropist Leopold Meyer stands at the far left. (MSS 157-540, Courtesy HMRC, Houston Public Library.)

The Shamrock's famous swimming pool, ca. 1949. The Shamrock's pool, at 165 feet by 142 feet, was advertised as the largest hotel pool in the nation. The pool was so large that water-skiing shows were performed there in the hotel's early years. It came complete with a three-tiered, Moderne-style diving board. (Courtesy Bob Bailey Studios Photographic Archive, CN 11921, The Center for American History, The University of Texas at Austin.)

This view of the Shamrock Hotel's pool shows the popular lanai unit in the background, a poolside addition to the Shamrock that was completed by Wyatt C. Hedrick in 1957. (Shamrock Hilton Booklet, Shamrock Hotel Vertical File, Courtesy HMRC, Houston Public Library.)

The Shamrock's massive size is apparent in this aerial photograph taken soon after the hotel's completion in 1949. (Brochstein's Inc. Shamrock Hotel Presentation Book, Shamrock Hotel Vertical File, Courtesy HMRC, Houston Public Library.)

Glen McCarthy's beloved hotel became the Shamrock Hilton following its sale to Conrad Hilton's chain in 1955. A higher-than-expected room vacancy rate, coupled with McCarthy's declining financial situation, forced him to make the sale. (MSS 157-532, Courtesy HMRC, Houston Public Library.)

The Streamlined Moderne reception desk was the focal point of the Shamrock's entrance lobby. (Brochstein's Inc. Shamrock Hotel Presentation Book, Shamrock Hotel Vertical File, Courtesy HMRC, Houston Public Library.)

Two Shamrock guests dine in the Emerald Room, 1949. The waiters shown in this photo were part of the 1,200-member staff employed at the hotel when it opened. (Courtesy Bob Bailey Studios Photographic Archive, CN 11929, The Center for American History, The University of Texas.)

The Cork Club, well known for its elaborate banquets, 1949. (Courtesy Bob Bailey Studios Photographic Archive, CN 11922, The Center for American History, The University of Texas at Austin.)

The Shamrock Hotel's demolition on June 1, 1987. Prior to the demolition, approximately three thousand persons demonstrated to save the Shamrock from destruction. At that time, it was the largest pro-preservation rally in Houston's history, but protesters' pleas were ignored. (Shamrock Hotel Vertical File, Courtesy HMRC, Houston Public Library.)

Battlestein's Department Store

Interior of Battlestein's Department Store, 2010 South Shepherd, ca. 1950. This suburban Battlestein's was designed by Joseph Finger who also designed earlier downtown incarnations of Battlestein's. The store's interior was reminiscent of Foley's Department Store, which opened in 1947. (Courtesy Bob Bailey Studios Photographic Archive, CN 11923, The Center for American History, The University of Texas.)

—— Sears, Roebuck and Co. Store ——

The first major department store built outside of Houston's downtown area was the Sears, Roebuck and Co. Department Store, located at Montrose and Allen Parkway. The store opened in 1926 but was vacated after water reached the store's second floor during the destructive 1935 flood. Sears then moved to a location on South Main. For many years the building served as a storage warehouse, but in its final days, it stood forlornly at the edge of a major apartment complex, the Bel Air, completed in 2006. The building of the complex was another element of a large-scale attempt by real estate interests to redevelop the beautiful acreage along Allen Parkway between downtown and the beginning of River Oaks. The old Sears store's proximity to the new wave of development placed it in great danger of being demolished, although the owners publicly claimed that they wanted to adapt the building for reuse rather than destroy it. In 2007, the building was finally demolished.

The Sears, Roebuck and Co. Department Store shortly after its opening in 1926. (Courtesy Bob Bailey Studios Photographic Archive, CN 11925, The Center for American History, The University of Texas.)

— Houston Turn-Verein Clubhouse —

This building housed Houston's oldest German-American fraternal organization, the Turn-Verein, founded in 1854. Designed by architect Joseph Finger, the Turn-Verein Clubhouse stood at 5502 Almeda Road and was completed in 1928 to mark the club's seventy-fifth anniversary. An acknowledged local Art Moderne landmark, the building was destroyed in 1993, despite many efforts to halt the demolition. A Walgreen's Drug Store now occupies the site. (MSS 97-90, Courtesy HMRC, Houston Public Library.)

Detail of stonework ornamentation on the Turn-Verein's exterior. Joseph Finger employed stylized floral Art Nouveau reliefs as a decorative motif. (MSS 97-86, Courtesy HMRC, Houston Public Library.)

An eagle sat atop the clubhouse entrance above the inscription "Turn-Verein." Various Art Nouveau patterns were used for ornamentation beneath the eagle. A set of nine bowling pins is also depicted, a reference to one of the members' favorite sports as well as to the Turn-Verein's bowling alley. (MSS 97-76, Courtesy HMRC, Houston Public Library.)

— San Jacinto Park —

Aerial Swing, San Jacinto Park, HOUSTON, Texas.

Park goers enjoy San Jacinto Park's enormous aerial swing, ca. 1910. San Jacinto Park was located on Houston Avenue, just north of White Oak Bayou. (MSS 187-194, Courtesy HMRC, Houston Public Library.)

—— Levy Brothers Dry Goods Store ——

Exterior of Levy Brothers Dry Goods Store at 309 Main, ca. 1927. Levy Brothers Company was founded in 1887; this photo was probably taken during its fortieth anniversary. Levy Brothers was one of the earliest Houston department stores to cater to the tastes of Houston's rapidly growing middle-class population. By 1929, Levy's had expanded to a new, larger building, designed by Joseph Finger, located at Main and Walker. (MSS 200-410, Courtesy HMRC, Houston Public Library.)

Levy Brothers' Canterbury Lunch Room. Like other Houston department stores, Levy Brothers included in-house dining facilities for the benefit of store customers. (MSS 187-351, Courtesy HMRC, Houston Public Library.)

To celebrate Levy's fortieth anniversary in 1927, the store exhibited in its main show window an elaborate diorama detailing the history of Houston. (MSS 157-1098, Courtesy HMRC, Houston Public Library.)

— First City National Bank Banking Pavilion —

*Perspective rendering of First City National Bank's Banking Pavilion by Skidmore, Owings & Merrill, ca. 1960. The Banking Pavilion was completed in 1961. It was demolished in 1998, furthering a disturbing trend of destroying Houston's Modernist buildings before they reached the half-century mark. A parking garage now occupies the site. (*Bank of Tomorrow, First National Bank Booklet, First National Bank Vertical File, Courtesy HMRC, Houston Public Library.*)*

*Elevation perspective rendering of the Banking Pavilion's "motor bank" located at 1001 Main Street by Skidmore, Owings & Merrill, ca. 1960. (*The New Look in Motor Banks, *First National Bank Booklet, First National Bank Vertical File, Courtesy HMRC, Houston Public Library.)*

— Carnegie Library —

Carnegie Library (on left), corner of Main and McKinney. The library, constructed with Carnegie Foundation funds, was completed in 1904 and was headed by the City of Houston's first librarian, Julia Ideson. The library was formally known as the Houston Lyceum and Carnegie Library and was later demolished after a new library (the current Julia Ideson Building) was completed in 1926. The turreted structure to the right of the library is the former First Presbyterian Church, which was also demolished. (MSS 187-118, Courtesy HMRC, Houston Public Library.)

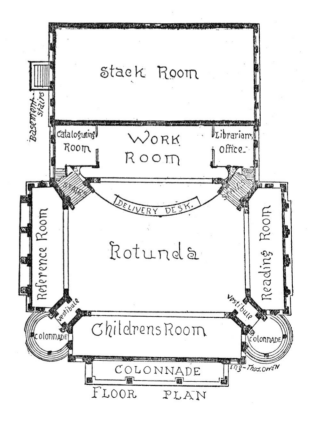

First floor plan, Carnegie Library, 1904. Note the basement stairs at upper left and the space allocated for cataloging and other types of daily library work. The small, cramped working spaces were one of the reasons Julia Ideson lobbied for the building of a new library, which was approved in 1924 and completed in 1926 at 500 McKinney Avenue. That structure remains standing and is known today as the Julia Ideson Building. ("Houston Library Reports 1904–1951," p. 18, Courtesy HMRC, Houston Public Library.)

LOST INTERIORS

THE BUILDINGS THAT follow represent an entirely different category of "Lost Houston." The exterior of these buildings remain standing, but their interiors—which represented a large part of their reputation—have either been altered beyond recognition or been gutted entirely and replaced with something far inferior to the original. In the case of the Sakowitz Department Store at 1111 Main, for example, the exterior, stripped of its signage and show windows, is still extant. However, the interior was entirely gutted and replaced with a parking garage. Few people would argue that a multilevel parking garage is any substitute for what were once some of the most lavish interiors ever designed for an American department store. An empty shell of a building, bereft of its interior design, hardly constitutes preservation. Houstonians must be aware that the loss of historically significant building interiors is often just as much an historical tragedy as the demolition of the entire structure. These photographs of Houston's "Lost Interiors" remind us that Houston once claimed some of the most beautifully designed, carefully crafted building interiors in the nation.

—— Sakowitz Brothers Store ——

SAKOWITZ BROTHERS STORE moved from 311 Main Street to a location at 712 Main within the Gulf Building, designed by Alfred Finn, in 1928. Although the Gulf Building, an Art Deco masterpiece, fortunately remains standing, the elaborate interiors that constituted the Sakowitz store are lost forever. The following photos and renderings give some idea of the Art Moderne quality of this high-end department store, with some of the most beautiful interiors ever designed for Houston merchandising. Kenneth Franzheim, who later gained fame as the architect of the downtown Foley's Department Store, served as a consulting architect for Alfred Finn's office. At that time, Franzheim was working in New York City, and one of his associates, J. E. R. Carpenter, also worked as a consulting architect on the Sakowitz Brothers Department Store.

Interior perspective drawing of Sakowitz Brothers Department Store, 1928. (MSS 19-351, Courtesy HMRC, Houston Public Library.)

Detail of Sakowitz arcade show window, 1928. (MSS 19-353, Courtesy HMRC, Houston Public Library.)

Perspective rendering of arcade show window, 1928. (MSS 19-352, Courtesy HMRC, Houston Public Library.)

Group portrait of Sakowitz Brothers hosiery sales staff showing some of the store's elaborate sales displays. (Courtesy Bob Bailey Studios Photographic Archive Collection, CN 11785, The Center for American History, University of Texas.)

This elegantly executed arcade show window featured Hanes hosiery. (Courtesy Bob Bailey Studios Photographic Archive, CN 11784, The Center for American History, The University of Texas.)

Ladies' accessories department, Sakowitz Brothers. (MSS 19-856, Courtesy HMRC, Houston Public Library.)

Ladies' shoe salon, Sakowitz Brothers. Note the intricate detailing on the grillwork and lighting fixtures. (MSS 19-862, Courtesy HMRC, Houston Public Library.)

Exterior view of Sakowitz Brothers entrance in the Gulf Building location at 712 Main. The photograph shows the Gulf Building's beautiful exterior ornamentation, which still survives. (MSS 19-1977, Courtesy HMRC, Houston Public Library.)

Another view of Sakowitz Brothers' exterior showing the store's corner and the elegantly appointed show windows that attracted passersby. (MSS 19-1676, Courtesy HMRC, Houston Public Library.)

— Sakowitz Department Store, 1111 Main —

IN 1951, SAKOWITZ BROTHERS moved again, this time to 1111 Main in a prime location directly across from the recently completed Foley's Department Store. It was the last of the major department stores to be built at a downtown location. Meant to compete with the sleek modernity of the award-winning Foley's Department Store, Sakowitz Brothers (the "Brothers" was dropped in the 1950s so that the store was simply named "Sakowitz") again hired Alfred Finn as their architect. The Sakowitz family was forced to close all of their stores beginning in the mid-1980s, and the downtown location was sold. While the exterior edifice of the building still stands, the interior of the building was gutted years ago and reconfigured as a parking garage, which is still in operation. Not a trace remains of the store's sumptuous interiors, for which no expense was spared. The signage on the building's exterior has also been removed.

Artist's rendering of Sakowitz Brothers, ca. 1950. (MSS 19-455, Courtesy HMRC, Houston Public Library.)

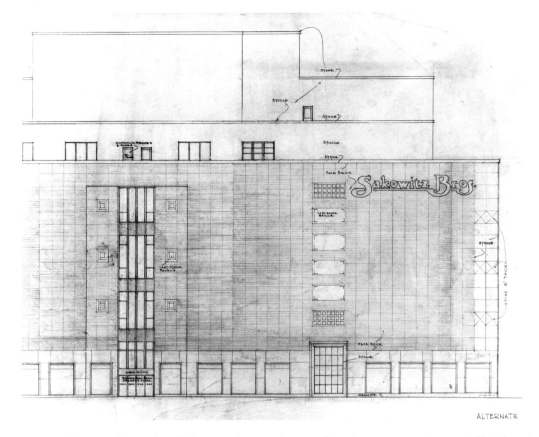

Architectural elevation drawing by Alfred Finn's office, 1950. (MSS 19-Job 565 Courtesy HMRC, Houston Public Library.)

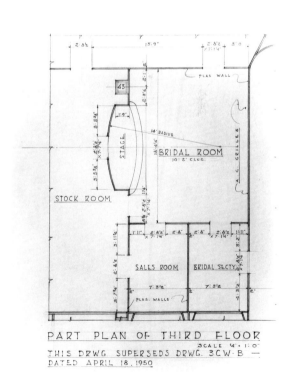

Partial plan of third floor showing location of bridal salon, 1950.
(MSS 19-Job 565, Courtesy HMRC, Houston Public Library.)

Interior shot of the bridal salon, 1951. (MSS 19-474, Courtesy HMRC, Houston Public Library.)

Sakowitz Brothers after completion, ca. 1951. (MSS 19-460, Courtesy HMRC, Houston Public Library.)

The men's ties and accessories department, ca. 1951. The interior photographs of the newly completed Sakowitz impart some idea of the store's spacious and elegant shopping areas. (MSS 19-513, Courtesy HMRC, Houston Public Library.)

Entrance to women's clothing and accessories, ca. 1951. (MSS 19-471, Courtesy HMRC, Houston Public Library.)

Fabrics and materials department, ca. 1951. (MSS 19-514, Courtesy HMRC, Houston Public Library.)

A beautiful mural depicting shapely sprites engaged in a variety of activities decorated the wall above the candy counter, ca. 1951. (MSS 19-476, Courtesy HMRC, Houston Public Library.)

Ladies' hats department, ca. 1951. (MSS 19-475, Courtesy HMRC, Houston Public Library.)

One of Sakowitz's elegant restaurants, ca. 1951. The fountain, potted plants, and faux trees were designed to give diners an outdoors feel while still providing them with the sense of style appropriate for a Sakowitz shopping experience. (MSS 19-495, Courtesy HMRC, Houston Public Library.)

Tower Theatre

The Tower Theatre, ca. 1972, a few years before its conversion to a live theatrical venue. The Tower, which opened in 1937, was another "suburban" theater built by the Interstate Theatres chain for the Montrose area. The Art Deco theater was designed by W. Scott Dunne. The Tower served as a space for private nightclubs during the 1980s after live stage productions like The Best Little Whorehouse in Texas *proved to be unprofitable. Still later the Tower became a Hollywood Video store, which still occupies the site. During the conversion process, the beautiful interiors were completely gutted and today only the Tower's altered exterior remains with the marquee now reading "Hollywood." Some of the adjacent stores, designed by MacKie & Kamrath during 1946–1950 in a similar style, are still occupied by retailers. (MSS 97-54, Courtesy HMRC, Houston Public Library.)*

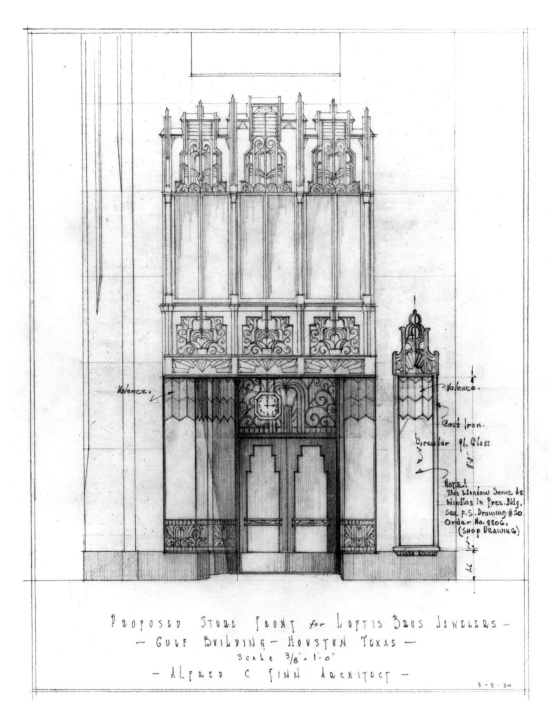

Proposed store front perspective drawing by Alfred Finn for Loftis Bros. Jewelry, 1930. Loftis Bros. Jewelry also occupied retail space inside the Gulf Building, which, luckily, is still extant. The beautiful interior of Loftis Brothers, however, has been lost. (MSS 19-Job 406, Courtesy HMRC, Houston Public Library.)

In the sketch: SKETCH NEW STORE / Loftis Bros. Jewelers / Gulf Bldg. Houston, Texas.

Sketch for interior of Loftis Bros. store by Alfred Finn, 1930. (MSS 19-Job 406, Courtesy HMRC, Houston Public Library.)

—— Rice Hotel ——

Saving the historic Rice Hotel from demolition was one of the more notable highlights for historic preservationists during the 1990s. Developer Randall Davis engineered the redevelopment of the vacant property, located at 909 Texas Avenue at Main Street, with the intention of converting the shuttered hotel into a downtown living space. While the exterior remains basically the same, only a portion of the original interiors are still extant, as the building had to be almost completely gutted and reconfigured in order to make suitably sized loft apartments for potential buyers and renters.

These photographs impart some idea of the Rice Hotel's interiors when the third incarnation of the hotel, designed by the St. Louis firm of Mauran, Russell & Crowell opened in 1912 under the ownership of Jesse H. Jones. Alfred Finn added another seventeen-story wing to the Rice Hotel's west side during 1925–1926 to complete the structure we see today. The renovated hotel is currently known as the Rice Lofts, which opened for business in 1998 and contains 312 units. Fortunately developers saved and restored the Rice's famous ballroom, the beautiful reception lobby, and its indoor swimming pool.

The third version of the Rice Hotel as it looked after its completion in 1912. Alfred Finn would later add another wing in 1926 to this U-shaped design by the St. Louis partnership of Mauran, Russell & Crowell. The Rice Hotel is located on the site where the capitol of the Republic of Texas was located during 1837–1839 and for a brief period in 1842. (MSS 19-792, Courtesy HMRC, Houston Public Library.)

Prior to the completion of Finn's addition, this earlier Rice Hotel Annex was constructed next door to the main hotel. The Annex contained a variety of services for guests, including a grocery store and barbershop. (MSS 1248-3493, Courtesy HMRC, Houston Public Library.)

The Rice Hotel's billiard room, ca. 1925. (MSS 19-1445, Courtesy HMRC, Houston Public Library.)

One of the Rice Hotel's rooms, ca. 1925, which was quite small by the standards of today's hotel rooms. (MSS 19-1443, Courtesy HMRC, Houston Public Library.)

One of the Rice Hotel's several restaurants and clubs, decorated with dark wood paneling, ca. 1925. A small circulating fan can be seen in the upper right-hand corner. Although the Rice Hotel cafeteria became the first air-conditioned facility in Texas in 1922, the entire hotel was not fully air-conditioned until many years later. (MSS 19-1429, Courtesy HMRC, Houston Public Library.)

Rice Hotel lobby and reception desk, ca. 1920. (MSS 19-1425, Courtesy HMRC, Houston Public Library.)

Foley's Department Store

Although the former Foley's Department Store remains standing and is still used by Macy's, virtually nothing remains of the original interiors. Even the top five of the store's ten floors are now sealed off to the public. A notable exception is the escalators, which, with forty-eight-inch wide steps, were the widest in the world when the store opened in 1947. Raymond Loewy, possibly America's most famous designer, was responsible for most of the interior design. Loewy promised that he would produce "entirely new architectural forms."[2] The store had 5,619 different types of lighting fixtures, to give just one example of the work that Loewy expended on the store. Foley's was a futuristic marvel when the store was completed. During opening day ceremonies, held on October 20, 1947, Foley's president Max Levine remarked to the thousands of people in attendance that Foley's was "the finest department store that architectural skill and engineering could devise."[3] Foley's was the first entirely new department store to open in the United States since the beginning of the Great Depression in 1929.[4]

One of the elaborate Christmas window displays that made downtown Foley's Department Store a tourist attraction in its own right each holiday season for many years after the store opened in 1947. A mainstay for spectacular theme displays was the 105-foot wide "vista window" located at the Main Street entrance. The huge show windows, especially designed for large displays, are now mostly boarded up. (Courtesy Bob Bailey Studios Photographic Archive, CN 11778, The Center for American History, The University of Texas.)

Foley's window displays were notable local attractions at any time of the year, although Christmas garnered the largest crowds. The sheer size of the show windows made the displays stand apart from other Houston department stores. With the accompanying artistry of the window dressers, shown in this dreamlike display of women's fur coats, Foley's windows were guaranteed to attract passersby. The neon sign of the Lamar Hotel, located across the street, is reflected on the right-hand side of the window. (Courtesy Bob Bailey Studios Photographic Archive, CN 11783, The Center for American History, The University of Texas.)

This photograph of Foley's first floor during the Christmas season of 1947 gives an idea of Loewy's original interior design, which emphasized functionality in its sleekness and accessibility. (Courtesy Bob Bailey Studios Photographic Archive, CN 11781, The Center for American History, The University of Texas.)

The "Crusade For Freedom" display was mounted on the first floor of Foley's in 1950. Customers were encouraged to sign a Freedom Scroll to help combat communism, and thousands of people complied during the exhibit's first week alone. The display is a wonderful example of how consumerism was tied to anticommunism in the minds of customers. (Courtesy Bob Bailey Studios Photographic Archive, CN 11779, The Center for American History, The University of Texas.)

One of several restaurants in Foley's catering to the legions of women shoppers who frequented the store, 1947. (Courtesy Bob Bailey Studios Photographic Archive, CN 11782, The Center for American History, The University of Texas.)

In 1950, Foley's fiftieth anniversary display in the store's huge vista window showed the Houston skyline in the year 2000. The model's 194 miniature cars, trains, and airplanes were motorized and moved around the display. This is another example of Houston's fascination with predictions about the twenty-first century. The display bears a remarkable resemblance to the model city of the future constructed for the General Motors 1956 promotional film, Design for Dreaming. *(MSS 157-325, Courtesy HMRC, Houston Public Library.)*

—— Astrodome (Harris County Domed Stadium) ——

WITH HARRIS COUNTY intent on redeveloping the famed Astrodome, no matter which conversion plan ultimately takes shape, there is absolutely no doubt that the original interior design that helped make the structure one of the engineering marvels of the twentieth century will be gutted. One of the current plans calls for conversion of the Dome, labeled the "Eighth Wonder of the World" at the time of its construction, into a grandiose convention hotel, complete with waterways and waterfalls. Plans also call for greatly altering the exterior by adding an enormous parking garage that will wrap around two-thirds of the Dome. Another plan, advocated by a sizable and vocal group of citizens, calls for razing the entire structure and using the surface as an enormous parking lot for patrons of the new Reliant Stadium next door. With support for the hotel project dwindling, discussions regarding other possible uses for the Dome continue to proliferate, including its possible use as a movie studio.

The first fully enclosed and fully air-conditioned sports stadium in the world, the pioneering Astrodome opened in April 1965. The Domed Stadium was renovated during the late 1980s when the number of seats was increased and massive pedestrian ramps were attached to its sides. In addition, the Dome's famous animated scoreboard was also removed. In any event, the Astrodome interiors that helped to put Houston on the map in the 1960s will be gone forever once the next "renovation" occurs. Sadly, this will happen despite the Astrodome's recent designation as a National Historic Civil Engineering Landmark.

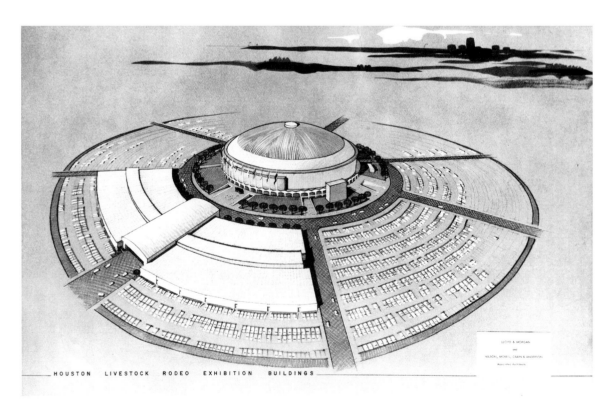

HOUSTON   LIVESTOCK   RODEO   EXHIBITION   BUILDINGS

Aerial perspective rendering of the Astrodome showing adjacent exhibition buildings constructed for the Houston Livestock Show and Rodeo, ca. 1962. The Astrodome architects were the firms of Lloyd & Morgan and Wilson, Morris, Crain & Anderson. (MSS 67-645, Courtesy HMRC, Houston Public Library.)

Astrodome during construction, ca. 1964. (RG D6-1216, Courtesy HMRC, Houston Public Library.)

Interior view looking south toward moveable field-level seats, ca. 2003. (SC 1433-12, Courtesy HMRC, Houston Public Library.)

Interior view looking east from one of the Astrodome's "sky boxes," ca. 2003. (SC 1433-11, Courtesy HMRC, Houston Public Library.)

View from cupola, ca. 2003. (SC 1433-16, Courtesy HMRC, Houston Public Library.)

Looking south toward moveable seats, ca. 2003. (SC 1433-09, Courtesy HMRC, Houston Public Library.)

Interior perspective view showing Astrodome field configured for a football game, ca. 2003. (SC 1433-10, Courtesy HMRC, Houston Public Library.)

Aerial view of the "Astrodomain" complex showing the Astrodome and the adjacent 104-acre Astroworld amusement park, ca. 1969. Astroworld was completed in 1968 and was a favorite playground for hundreds of thousands of Houstonians for more than a quarter century. The park was purchased by Six Flags in 1975, sold to real estate developers in 2005, and demolished in 2006. No sign of the huge amusement park remains today; all that is left is a vacant field with a few scattered pieces of iron, brick, and wood left over from the demolition. (MSS 243-685, Courtesy HMRC, Houston Public Library.)

NOTES

1. Karl Kamrath, interview, transcript, Karl Kamrath Vertical File, HMRC.

2. Loewy, *Never Leave Well Enough Alone*, 202.

3. Mary E. Johnston, "Excited Throng Pours in After Noon Ceremony," *Houston Post*, n.d.

4. Sam Boenig, "The Story of Foley's—From $2000 Store to one of Nation's Best," *Houston Post*, sec.3, January 29, 1950.

II

UNBUILT

★ ★

HOUSTON

INTRODUCTION

"With cities, it is as with dreams:
everything imaginable can be dreamed."
—ITALO CALVINO, *INVISIBLE CITIES*

SINCE THE DAWN OF recorded history and literature, humans have been fascinated with unbuilt architectural projects. The tale of the Tower of Babel from the first book of the Old Testament is one of the most frequently represented stories. As recorded in Genesis 11:3–8 (King James Version):

> 3: And they said one to another, Go to, let us make brick, and burn them thoroughly. And they had brick for stone, and slime had they for morter. 4: And they said, Go to, let us build us a city and a tower, whose top may reach unto heaven; and let us make us a name, lest we be scattered abroad upon the face of the whole earth. 5: And the Lord came down to see the city and the tower, which the children builded. 6: And the Lord said, Behold, the people is one, and they have all one language; and this they begin to do: and now nothing will be restrained from them, which they have imagined to do. 7: Go to, let us go down, and there confound their language, that they may not understand one another's speech. 8: So the Lord scattered them abroad from thence upon the face of all the earth: and they left off to build the city.

With no visuals to guide them, artists' imaginations run wild in their portrayals of how the doomed city and its accompanying tower must have looked. Over the centuries, from psalters in medieval times to the works of Pieter Bruegel the Elder in the Renaissance and Gustav Doré in the nineteenth century, the partially completed Tower of Babel has been portrayed as massive ziggurats, step pyramids with terraced gardens, conical minaret-like structures, and fanciful edifices reminiscent of great buildings of classical antiquity. Aside from the obvious moral of the story—mortals should avoid hubristic acts that God might interpret as overstepping their bounds—and its accompanying explanation of the world's linguistic and cultural differences, the story of Nimrod's thwarted high-rise became symbolic of what architects might achieve, if they were sure to stop short of actually trying to reach heaven. Until the nineteenth century, the Tower of Babel remained in the collective unconscious of the Western world the archetypal example of an unbuilt architectural project and served as an inspiration to any builder or architect with lofty aspirations. As late as 1935, *American Weekly* magazine published an article entitled, "Science Plans New Tower of Babel Six Miles High."

The Greeks and Romans had their own unbuilt schemes, but since there is no surviving architectural or engineering documentation in the form of drawings or models these are largely known only through ancient literature. The Roman architect Vitruvius wrote that Alexander the Great's personal architect, Dinocrates, proposed carving a statue into the face of a Greek mountain in honor of Alexander. The carving, which would have portrayed a seated Alexander, was intended to be so enormous that Alexander's left hand would hold a city large enough for 10,000 residents and a river would have flowed from his right hand into the Aegean Sea. Alexander's untimely death halted the project.

By the Middle Ages, some architects and builders were using three-dimensional models and architectural drawings onsite, particularly during construction of the great Gothic cathedrals. The use of three-dimensional architectural renderings, sometimes attributed to the artist Raphael who used such renderings while working on St. Peter's Basilica, meant that there were finally visual representations of unbuilt projects that could help non-architects envision the completed structure. The population explosion and rapid industrialization of the late eighteenth through the twentieth century led to an almost exponential increase in the size of cities. This expansion of urban areas and the resulting need for new buildings meant that there was now a proliferation of documented unbuilt projects. Some of these were ordinary, but others were grandiose, such as the utopian schemes of the French architect Claude-Nicholas Ledoux. Images of these unbuilt buildings grew in the consciousness and memories of humankind.

Over the past few decades, it has been something of a parlor game among architects and historians to speculate about what a city might have been like if proposed but unbuilt buildings had made it to the completion stage. Might the cityscape have been more beautiful today? Would the completion of a certain large-scale, mixed-use project have reoriented the city's later growth patterns? If a proposed housing project had been completed, would it have slowed the spread of blighted slums near the city's core? If a greenbelt around the city's perimeter had been finished three decades ago, would it have inspired people to become more aware of the recreational and environmental benefits that green spaces can bring? The perennial "What if?" architectural guessing game had extended to many members of the general public by the end of the twentieth century. Architectural exhibits based on the "unbuilt" theme have been held worldwide in cities as diverse as Melbourne, Australia, and Cincinnati, Ohio. Architect Leon van Schaik has aptly summarized the impact of this kind of speculation about our unbuilt environment: "Unbuilt architecture congregates in the imagination of its creators, and of historians, and critics, aggregating into the secret cities of the mind."[1]

Aside from the speculation that fantasizing about unbuilt projects might engender, there is an equally valid, practical aspect to such an exercise. For historians, the buildings that a city decides *not* to build often offer as much insight into the minds and psyche of a city's population at a given time as do the buildings that were actually completed. What do the following photographs of some of Houston's unbuilt buildings tell us about the

nature of the city? In virtually every instance, Houston's unbuilt buildings project an unwavering sense of optimism for the future and a strong faith in technology.

Unlike the lost buildings of the preceding section, the buildings shown in the following illustrations never made it past the planning stages. Sometimes the conceived building never made it past a single rendering an architect made to present to a client. At other times, huge sums of money were spent on planning; occasionally, land was even purchased for the project. These building proposals were usually the victims of economic recessions or depressions or a loss of funding due to the outbreak of war. At times these proposals remained unbuilt simply because a client changed his mind, ran out of funds, or had a disagreement with the architect. In other instances, the proposals were simply too visionary stylistically. Not surprisingly, two of Houston's most prolific architects, Alfred Finn and Kenneth Franzheim, and one architectural firm, MacKie & Kamrath, are well represented in this selection of unbuilt buildings, simply because not only did they generate a good number of unbuilt proposals, but the historical documentation of their work has been preserved in archival collections.

Although the details of the projects and the reasons for their stoppage may differ, unbuilt projects hold a fascination in each major American city. Chicago has the Illinois, Frank Lloyd Wright's mile-high skyscraper, and numerous proposals for buildings that were never built for the 1893 and 1933 World's Fairs. The 1939–1940 World's Fair in New York presented science-fiction-like elevated highways running right through the upper reaches of skyscrapers, floating airports, and other futuristic urban visions. Houston, a city with money, exuberance, and energy to spare, has its own trove of unbuilt treasures. Once Houston embraced the pursuit of modernity, architects quickly saw the benefits of tying their work to advanced ideas and concepts, even in a city that was considered by most to be culturally conservative. As Houston's economy and population grew at an almost unchecked rate during the twentieth century, the increased rate of construction began to generate a number of architectural projects destined to remain unbuilt.

The February 9, 1964 issue of the now-defunct *Houston Post* featured a special section on what Houston would be like at the turn of the next century. Entitled "Houston Tomorrow: Leaders Project City Into the Year 2000," the section presented the predictions of a vari-

In this stylized sketch drawn in 1964, an artist for the Houston Post *envisioned the Port of Houston covered with a massive, hexagonal-paned dome. Beneath the honeycomb-like dome (presumably plastic-paned like the Astrodome), ships move and unload their cargoes along the Houston Ship Channel. (*Houston Post *(Supplement), "Houston Tomorrow: Leaders Project City Into the Year 2000," February 9, 1964, Courtesy HMRC, Houston Public Library.)*

ety of businessmen, educators, and other civic leaders. All respondents were male; not a single woman was included. Keeping in mind that the participants were only discussing thirty-four years into the future, the answers predicted a technological utopia with few restrictions on what Houstonians could achieve in a mere three decades. With the Astrodome then under construction, Howard Tellepsen, chairman of the Harris County Houston Ship Channel Navigation District, predicted that the entire Port of Houston would be covered with a dome. After all, if an enormous stadium could be covered with a dome, what could possibly hinder similar projects in the future? As Tellepsen asks, "Why not a complete dome-covered port by the year 2000 where every day is a working day

and laborers load and unload ships impervious to heat and cold or rain?"[2] And, Tellepsen predicted that under the dome, atomic-powered ships would transit the Ship Channel to deliver the goods of the world to the Port of Houston, which had every possibility of becoming the largest port in the United States by 2000.

The president of Rapid Transit Lines, Inc., Bernard Calkins, predicted that atomic-powered buses would operate on air cushions within separated rights-of-way down Houston streets. Calkins assured readers that "undoubtedly" downtown Houston would be "a complete air-conditioned mall."[3] In the realm of future communications, the general manager of Southwestern Bell confidently opined that commuters would no longer be driving their cars to their jobs by 2000, since all workers would be able to work from home by using large-screen "phonovision." This change in the work environment would also eliminate the traffic problems that others foresaw in the future, since working by phonovision would drastically reduce the number of cars on Houston's roads and highways.

Sometimes publicity for a particular project such as the Houston Center, proposed in the 1970s for the eastern side of downtown, was so extensive that even if the proposal remained unbuilt, it would remain implanted in the city's unconscious. Newspapers and local television news shows regularly featured photos of Houston Center renderings and architectural models to tout the size of the project and the benefits it would bring to Houston. (Any possible negatives about the project and its impact were never mentioned, of course.) As the representations of Houston Center proliferated in the media, they began to acquire a life of their own, confirming urbanist Mark Wigley's belief that, "Modern architecture is inseparable from the logic of the photographed model."[4] Years after the project was canceled, one of my university professors asked me how Houston Center was coming along and if the builders were maintaining their schedule.

There has been a frequent tendency in architectural circles to bemoan the loss of unbuilt projects, as though each one would have been some sort of architectural gem contributing to the improvement of the built environment. This is hardly the case. Aside from the fact that some unbuilt proposals were staggeringly impractical and their conceptualization inept, several of the unbuilt project designs were simply ugly. Still others would have wreaked environmental havoc on a city already saddled with enormous pollution problems. The increased automobile traffic that the Houston Center would have engendered and the pollutants that would have been trapped by a proposed dome over the Port of Houston immediately come to mind.

While we can oftentimes salute the architectural imagination and creativity that devised certain unbuilt projects, the fact that some of them remained unfinished is hardly a loss to either Houston or, more generally, architecture. On the other hand, the quality designs of some of the proposals would have enhanced Houston's cityscape and possibly contributed to the betterment of the city's environment. Although the failure to complete some of the far-sighted, well-designed buildings can correctly be seen as a loss, merely seeing the images of some of these visionary unbuilt structures still speaks to the utopian impulse in each of us. At the very least, Houston's unbuilt buildings reflect the energy and unbridled optimism of the city that inspired them.

NOTES

1. Leon van Schaik, introduction to *Melbourne's Unseen Might-Have Beens Exhibition: Unbuilt Projects Catalogue*, by Royal Australian Institute of Architecture, Victoria Chapter, 1987.

2. Howard Tellepsen, "A Network of Ship Channels Leading to Gulf and Inland." *Houston Post*, Supplement, February 9, 1964.

3. Bernard E. Calkins, "Calkins Foresees Cushion of Air, Atomic Power Bus." *Houston Post*, Supplement, February 9, 1964.

4. Casebere and Seator, 16.

IMAGES

—— Houston Center (Texas Eastern Project) ——

No other unbuilt project symbolizes the "Houston that Never Was" more than the Texas Eastern Transmission Corporation's Houston Center, intended for construction on the east side of downtown but never realized. The sheer scale and audacity of the proposed Houston Center still inspires awe, as it would have been the single largest privately financed construction project in American history, surpassing Rockefeller Center and doubling the size of Houston's central business district. First proposed in 1970, Houston Center had lost support by the late 1970s due in large part to steady inflation and a sharp economic recession. Although Houston Center was typical of Houston's "can-do" attitude at the time it was announced, its demise coincided with the decline of future-oriented optimism in American society. An ignominious end to the U.S.'s involvement in the Vietnam War in 1975, two economic downturns in the same decade, fuel shortages, and inflation all contributed to a national sense of malaise.

Houston Center was projected to cover an area of thirty-three city blocks, or seventy-four acres. Plans called for the completion of Houston Center to be carried out in three phases, with construction of Phase One scheduled to begin in November 1971. The Phase One portion alone was scheduled to contain five million square feet of office space. If all three phases had been completed, the Center would have had twenty-three million square feet of office space. In essence, Houston Center was a multilevel "platform city," apart from the rest of Houston's flat grid pattern, although every effort was to be made to integrate the project into Houston's existing urban fabric. Despite the public statements by Texas Eastern officials that Houston Center would blend in with the rest of Houston, the developers were basically attempting to create an almost totally different environment within the Center's confines. Referring to

the platform city concept, one journalist gushed that at last Houston would have its own Acropolis.

Press releases touted the Center's advantages for a wider audience than just Houston: "With its unique pedestrian-centered design and its mechanical movement systems, Houston Center might well provide the model solution to present and future traffic handling in urban areas."[1] Although the initial plans for Houston Center called for a people mover system within the Center, the primary transportation remained the automobile. Parking spaces for 40,000–50,000 cars and a new system of elevated roads were planned for Houston Center. This emphasis on the automobile was pragmatic for Houston, but belied any futuristic aura that Texas Eastern tried to convey about the project.

As the 1970s wore on, schedules fell further and further behind. In addition, after only a few years, the plans for Houston Center had been downsized considerably. The idea for a platform city was abandoned in favor of a pair of run-of-the-mill skyscraper office complexes. Two Houston Center was completed by 1974, an unimpressive high-rise building that was eventually paired with One Houston Center, completed four years later. Texas Eastern representatives, who cited "extreme inflationary construction costs" as the primary reason for the drastic revision of plans,[2] were nervous that Houstonians were unaware of the reduced-scale changes for Houston Center because the media continued to use drawings illustrating the initial platform city concept even after the original plans were jettisoned. Nonetheless, as late as 1976, some Texas Eastern publicity releases continued to insist that the 1970 grand plan would ultimately be implemented. By the end of the decade, it was clear that the original Houston Center would never be built.

If the film-like, matte painting quality of the illustrations of Houston Center that follow remind you of the futuristic city featured in the film *Logan's Run* (1976), they should. The architect of Houston Center, Los Angeles-based William Pereira, was a great fan of science fiction and his work with the proposed Center's design allowed his imagination to roam freely. In addition, Pereira had worked in the film industry before becoming an architect, and he won an Academy Award for his assistance with the scenic effects of *Reap the Wild Wind* (1942). Finally, Pereira also loved racing cars, making him a sympathetic architect for car-oriented Houston.

This aerial photograph of downtown Houston looking west shows the footprint of the proposed Houston Center. Dallas Avenue, on the left side of the photo, marked the southern boundary of the project, which would have extended eastward as far as the elevated portion of the Eastex Freeway (U.S. 59). The westernmost boundary of Houston Center was planned for an area near the intersection of Fannin and McKinney. Rusk Avenue marked the northern boundary. (Houston Center Vertical File, Courtesy HMRC, Houston Public Library.)

Rendering of covered street intended to be completed during the first phase of Houston Center's construction. In this scene, pedestrians stroll along the ground level, with parking garages above. The parking garages are ventilated, and the roof of the garages' highest levels provides another pedestrian walkway with additional stores and services. The architects and developers often emphasized any human-scale qualities that Houston Center provided in order to counter the arguments of critics that the massive size of the project made it seem cold and impersonal. (Houston Center Vertical File, Courtesy HMRC, Houston Public Library.)

Concept drawing of one of Houston Center's numerous planned pedestrian malls located either within or adjacent to high-rise office buildings. A people mover system, intended for use within Houston Center, glides along its elevated track on the right side of the rendering. (Houston Center Vertical File, Courtesy HMRC, Houston Public Library.)

Aerial perspective drawing of Houston Center's Phase One core looking east. (MSS 157-917, Courtesy HMRC, Houston Public Library.)

A closer view of Houston Center's Phase One epicenter, with parking garages and retail/pedestrian malls in forefront. The circular building on the right is a 1,000-room hotel. (Houston Center Vertical File, Courtesy HMRC, Houston Public Library.)

Architectural model of Phase One of the Houston Center complex. The elevated road in the model's fore-ground assists traffic movement solely within Houston Center. William L. Pereira & Associates constructed the model. (Houston Center Vertical File, Courtesy HMRC, Houston Public Library.)

Architect William Pereira (right) inspects the model of Houston Center's Phase One development. Pereira's two primary personal interests—science fiction and race cars—melded perfectly with the designs for Houston Center. (Houston Center Vertical File, Courtesy HMRC, Houston Public Library.)

Concept drawing for parking substructure of Houston Center. An early publicity release stated that "Houston Center will recognize the relationship of the automobile to the Central Business District by providing adequate parking within the project area." Four levels of parking were to be provided along the perimeter of the Phase One development. The master plan called for the eventual creation of 40,000–50,000 parking spaces. (Houston Center Vertical File, Courtesy HMRC, Houston Public Library.)

Artist's concept of people mover system moving above the main pedestrian level of Houston Center. Moving sidewalks (at bottom left) were planned to convey passengers to the people mover stations. Although the people mover system was initially intended for use entirely within Houston Center, plans were made to link the system with any people mover that might eventually be constructed in the Central Business District. (Houston Center Vertical File, Courtesy HMRC, Houston Public Library.)

Architect William Pereira stands before a concept drawing of the entire Houston Center that is superimposed on a photo of the then-extant surrounding areas of downtown Houston. This drawing imparts an idea of the project's massive size and scale. (Houston Center Vertical File, Courtesy HMRC, Houston Public Library.)

Aerial photograph of the proposed site for Houston Center on the eastern side of the Central Business District. (Houston Center Vertical File, Courtesy HMRC, Houston Public Library.)

Close-up view of Phase One development. This rendering was produced in order to show how Houston Center would relate to the existing street system. An early publicity release stated that "Structures along the perimeter will be designed so that the entire project will have a good relationship to adjacent property." (Houston Center Vertical File, Courtesy HMRC, Houston Public Library.)

Concept drawing showing "the relationship between hotel structures and low- and high-rise office space." The view is toward the west from about six levels above ground level. The cascading structures in the center were intended to be garden-type apartments, which would overlook broad pedestrian plazas. (Houston Center Vertical File, Courtesy HMRC, Houston Public Library.)

Sterling Hotel (Proposed)

This hotel proposal, probably one of entrepreneur Ross Sterling's many Houston-area real estate projects, is more reminiscent of midtown Manhattan in the 1920s than Houston. (MSS 187-348, Courtesy HMRC, Houston Public Library.)

Alfred Finn's office prepared this rendering in the 1920s for a massive, but ornately designed, department store. The tile work along the eaves suggests that this store would have been another addition to the many Mediterranean-style buildings that were constructed in Houston during this time period. Had several proposed Mediterranean-style buildings actually been completed during the 1920s, it would have helped to produce a more uniform architectural style throughout the city. (MSS 19-1409, Courtesy HMRC, Houston Public Library.)

Houston S.P.C.A. Building (Proposed)

SOCIETY FOR PREVENTION OF CRUELTY TO ANIMALS

*Architectural Modernism had so infused Houston by the mid-twentieth century that Kenneth Franzheim even used the style for this proposed A-framed building, ca. 1955, meant to serve as headquarters of the local Society for the Prevention of Cruelty to Animals (S.P.C.A.). (*Postwar Planning, *Franzheim, n.p. Courtesy HMRC, Houston Public Library.)*

Sketch of proposed entrance gate to Memorial Park, architect unknown. This graceful, modest gate leading into Memorial Park was proposed around the time of the park's acquisition by the City of Houston in 1924. (RG A18, Courtesy HMRC, Houston Public Library.)

Bank of the Southwest Tower (Proposed)

A major national competition was held in 1982 to select a design for the planned eighty-two-story Bank of the Southwest Tower, which would have become Houston's tallest building. The seventy-five-story J.P. Morgan Chase Tower, completed in 1981, currently holds this title. The winning design was submitted by the Chicago firm of Murphy/Jahn. The planning stages of the Southwest Tower occurred during Houston's serious economic downturn in the early 1980s, and lack of funding eventually killed the project, which had a cost estimate of $350–400 million. This rendering of downtown Houston at night shows the prominent position that the Bank of the Southwest Tower would have occupied in the Houston skyline. (MSS 157, uncataloged photograph, Courtesy HMRC, Houston Public Library.)

Main entrance of the Bank of the Southwest Tower, 1982. The high-rise was planned for the block bounded by Louisiana, Milam, Walker, and McKinney streets. (MSS 157, uncataloged photograph, Courtesy HMRC, Houston Public Library.)

Five proposals for the Bank of the Southwest Tower, 1982. With completion estimated for 1986, Time *magazine predicted that the tower "might give people a reason to come downtown, where the action is supposed to be." (MSS 157, uncataloged photograph, Courtesy HMRC, Houston Public Library.)*

The spire of the 1,360-foot Bank of the Southwest Tower, 1982. An observation deck and restaurant were planned for the tower's pinnacle. (MSS 157, uncataloged photograph, Courtesy HMRC, Houston Public Library.)

—— San Jacinto Monument ——

THE SAN JACINTO MONUMENT is so iconic in Texas, it is interesting to see four rejected proposals for the monument constructed to commemorate the centennial of the battle for Texas independence. The office of Alfred Finn, the architect of the existing monument, produced these proposal drawings.

This proposal for the monument clearly shows the influence of the Lincoln Memorial, complete with reflecting pool in the front and statue in the inner chamber. The Lincoln Memorial was finished in 1922 and was widely admired for its classical simplicity. Finn may have been trying to impart a similar feel for this memorial to Texas independence. (MSS 19-Job 443, Courtesy HMRC, Houston Public Library.)

PROPOSED SAN JACINTO MEMORIAL.

Another classical proposal, this one more akin to the George Rogers Clark Memorial in Vincennes, Indiana. The Clark Memorial was completed in 1933, just three years before work began on the San Jacinto Monument. Finn would have been aware of the memorial's construction because it was widely publicized in contemporary architectural journals. (MSS 19-Job 443, Courtesy HMRC, Houston Public Library.)

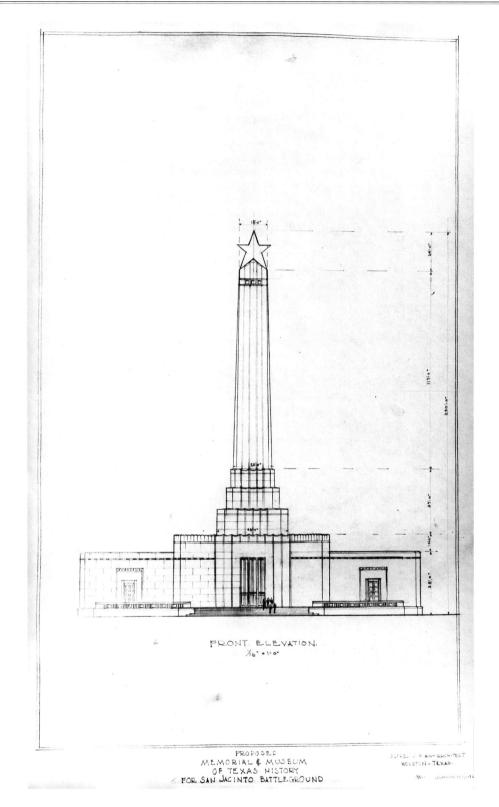

FRONT ELEVATION.
⅛⁶ = 1'-0"

PROPOSED
MEMORIAL & MUSEUM
OF TEXAS HISTORY
FOR SAN JACINTO BATTLEGROUND

*A proposal for a greatly reduced, scaled-down version of the design that was ultimately
selected. (MSS 19-Job 443, Courtesy HMRC, Houston Public Library.)*

This proposal also contains elements of the final design, but instead of a shaft rising from the Moderne base, Finn proposed a giant classical column crowned by a statue, most likely Sam Houston or an allegorical representation of victory. (MSS 19-Job 443, Courtesy HMRC, Houston Public Library.)

The San Jacinto Monument as it stands today, far more grandiose than any of the earlier proposals. No doubt Jesse H. Jones, who helped steer the monument to completion, thought this 570-foot behemoth (it really is 15 feet taller than the Washington Monument) was more fitting as a tribute to Texas independence. Completed in 1939, it remains the world's tallest war memorial. (MSS 19-658, Courtesy HMRC, Houston Public Library.)

CITY HALL.
HOUSTON, TEXAS.

Alfred Finn devised this proposal in 1927 for a new Houston City Hall to replace the existing Victorian-style City Hall, built in 1904. Although Finn's proposal precedes the beginning of officially sanctioned Stalinist architecture by several years, the building had roughly the same attraction as later Stalinist and German fascist megastructures and has all the charm of Moscow State University's high-rise central tower. The onset of the Great Depression in 1929 prevented the design from being completed. (Alfred Finn Vertical File, Courtesy HMRC, Houston Public Library.)

— Houston Exposition Center (Proposed) —

GEORGE KESSLER, THE famed St. Louis landscape architect and urban planner who helped design the St. Louis World's Fair of 1904, was invited to Houston in 1912. He worked on several park projects for the City of Houston, including the development of a master plan for Hermann Park that was largely ignored until recent years. One of Kessler's proposals was the development of the Houston Exposition Center, a sort of permanent, ongoing world's fair, to be located on the north bank of Buffalo Bayou (or Buffalo River, as Kessler designated it). Unfortunately, the arrival of World War I doomed any chances for Kessler to receive funding for his vision.

If Kessler's exposition grounds had been completed, Houston would have been able to claim a beautiful legacy from one of the nation's foremost landscape architects and city planners. The exposition would also have become yet another example of the strong commercial and civic ties between Houston and St. Louis, which was forged by the railroads. Other St. Louis architects who worked in Houston at the time included Mauran and Russell, who designed the 1912 incarnation of the Rice Hotel, the City Auditorium, and the DePelchin Faith Home, and Olle Lorehn, who originally came to the city to work on the American Brewery facility. Lorehn moved permanently to Houston in 1893, and became one of the city's leading architects.

Aerial perspective rendering showing the siting and layout of George Kessler's "Plan of Exposition."
(George Kessler Collection, Courtesy HMRC, Houston Public Library.)

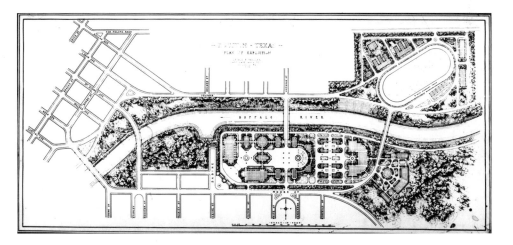

Site plan for George Kessler's Houston Exposition, located on the north bank of the "Buffalo River."
(George Kessler Collection, Courtesy HMRC, Houston Public Library.)

Convention Garden for Society of American Florists
and Ornamental Horticulturalists (Proposed)

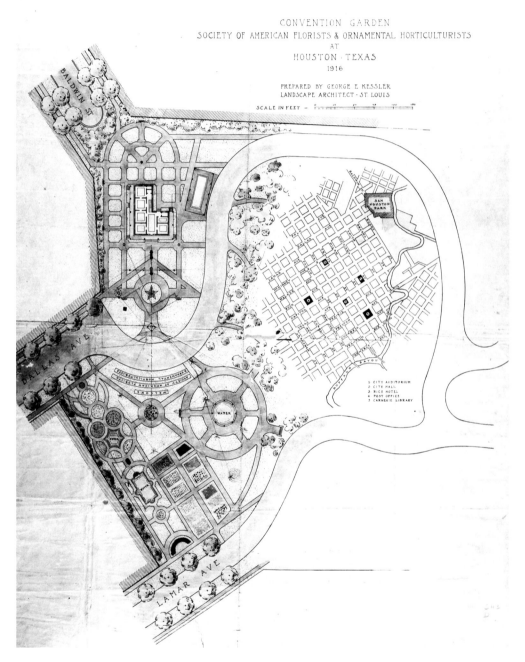

Layout and site plan for the Convention Garden by George Kessler, 1916. The original drawing was executed in watercolors. In 1916, Kessler also drew up plans for a "Convention Garden" for the Society of American Florists and Ornamental Horticulturalists annual convention, utilizing part of the grounds of Sam Houston Park at the foot of Baldwin Street and above Lamar Avenue. Sadly, like Kessler's Exposition Center, the beautifully designed garden, which was intended to welcome conventioneers, was also never implemented. (George Kessler Collection, Courtesy HMRC, Houston Public Library.)

Civic Center (Proposed)

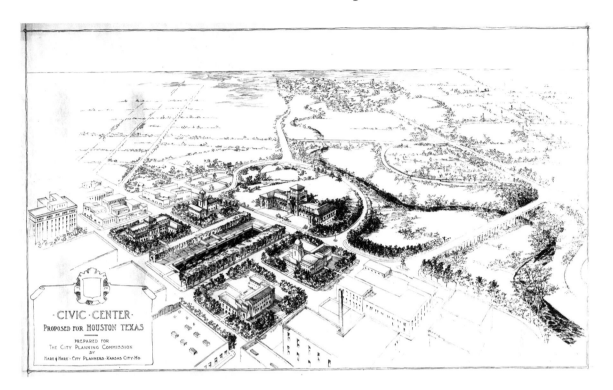

In 1926, the Kansas City landscape architecture firm of Hare & Hare was hired by the City of Houston to come up with a plan for an architecturally unified Civic Center. As envisioned, the proposed center would have buildings for both the City and Harris County. This aerial perspective shows that Hare & Hare proposed that the entire Civic Center be built in the same Mediterranean revival style that was used in the design of the Houston Public Library (now the Julia Ideson Building), which was completed the same year. Unfortunately, the harsh intervention of the Great Depression ruled out any building project on this scale. Sadly, it was Houston's lone chance to have a large cluster of structures built in a single style. Had the Civic Center been completed, Houston would have had a core of Mediterranean-style buildings as unified and perhaps as visually impressive as downtown Santa Barbara, California. (RG D26, Courtesy HMRC, Houston Public Library.)

This photo shows the general area intended for the construction of Hare & Hare's proposed Civic Center. Only the Houston Public Library at lower left was ever completed. The park across the street from the library, formally known as Martha Hermann Square, would later become the site for architect Joseph Finger's Art Moderne–style City Hall. (RG A13-3054, Courtesy HMRC, Houston Public Library.)

— Monorail System (Proposed) —

For the millions of American television viewers who tuned in every week to see *Disneyland* in the mid-to-late 1950s, few concepts symbolized the future of transportation like the monorail. The extensive publicity given to the monorail by Walt Disney was partially because Disney wanted to promote the monorail system he was installing in the Tomorrowland section of his Disneyland amusement park. But Disney, along with a host of other visionaries, also genuinely believed in the benefits that a monorail system could bring to heavily urbanized areas already choked with traffic congestion. Houston was one of the few cities in the world that came tantalizingly close to having its own monorail system (not once, but twice), and even had one of the few working models in the world outside of Disneyland itself. A little-known fact today is that Houston's prototype was the first monorail system to operate in the United States, even preceding Disneyland's monorail.

A fully operative, working monorail model was installed in Houston's Arrowhead Park on Old Spanish Trail. This photo was probably taken on opening day, February 18, 1956, when the 970-foot-line Skyway Trailblazer car was demonstrated to the press and public for the first time. (RG A-20 Folder 8, Courtesy HMRC, Houston Public Library.)

Houston's on-again, off-again dance with the monorail spanned three decades. Houston voters approved funding in 1988, and after several studies a monorail system was determined to be the best available alternative to further freeway construction. Then-mayor Kathy Whitmire gave her full backing to monorail transportation, but Whitmire was defeated in the 1991 mayoral election by Bob Lanier, who had made opposition to the monorail one of the cornerstones of his campaign. As a representative of traditional Houston business and real estate interests, Lanier had little use for a system that did not promote continued freeway construction and urban sprawl, which benefited Houston's power brokers. Thirty years after the monorail was first broached as a solution to Houston's transportation woes, Lanier administered the final blow to the transportation system that would have placed Houston in the forefront of urban mass transit, not only in the United States but also in the world.[3]

Interior shot showing the Trailblazer monorail car's seating arrangement. At the time, even the design of the chairs was considered ultra-modern for public transportation. (RG A20, Folder 8, Courtesy HMRC, Houston Public Library.)

Concept shot projecting what an elevated monorail stop would like at the Rice Hotel. Conceptual images such as this one were meant to show how new projects would integrate into a city's existing fabric. (RG A-20 Folder 8, Courtesy HMRC, Houston Public Library.)

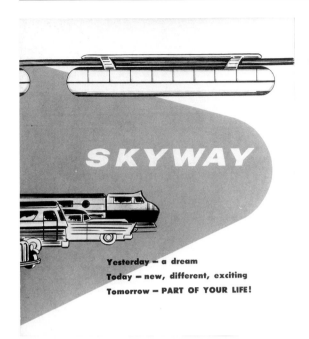

SKYWAY

Yesterday — a dream
Today — new, different, exciting
Tomorrow — PART OF YOUR LIFE!

Cover of a brochure distributed by Monorail Inc. to influential Houstonians. Monorail Inc. waged an intense campaign to promote the monorail in Houston. In this brochure, the Skyway monorail system is touted as the next logical step in the evolution of transportation, with the clear implication that rejection of the monorail meant that you were not aligning with the "tomorrow" of the future. (RG A20, Folder 8, Courtesy HMRC, Houston Public Library.)

Conceptual drawing from an advertisement for Rapid Transit Lines, Inc., Houston Post, *1964. This drawing suggests that in the future, passengers of the bus company would instead be carried by the elevated Rapid Transit Monorail system. ("Houston Tomorrow: Leaders Project City Into the Year 2000" (Supplement),* Houston Post, *February 9, 1964, Courtesy HMRC, Houston Public Library.)*

—— People Mover System ——

ANOTHER MASS TRANSIT system that was proposed for use in Houston was the people mover system, which would have been installed for use in the downtown central business district area in the late 1970s. The people mover system was similar to the monorail, but the cars were smaller and operated separately rather than being joined in train formation to help remove the aversion many Houstonians (and other Americans) had to mass transit. The Aerospace Corporation, based in Los Angeles, had conducted intensive, detailed studies for such a system during the 1970s, and had installed and operated a reduced-scale model. Although the Aerospace system was to be built in Los Angeles, there was little doubt of the system's viability in other locales, and the people mover was subsequently pitched to several cities, including Houston. Lack of public interest and funding led to the people mover perishing before it ever got off the drawing board. Although the people mover received extensive positive publicity in local media, the city once again rejected a rational transportation system in favor of more cars, freeways, and urban sprawl.

whether access is required from street level, or from a building, or both. This section presents a number of possible approaches to station and guideway design, and illustrates the flexibility afforded by the small scale of the new systems. The renderings included here are the station with the building it serves.

The downtown setting shown at left illustrates several architectural and industrial design concepts; it encompasses a typical section of guideway and an off-line station at a large department store. The guideway covers building structure. The station itself is off-line, and in this design vehicles are parked in it by lateral movement into a small area of the store's second floor.

Another approach to guideway design for the same location is illustrated above. In this case the guideway provides

In this artist's rendering, the people mover cars glide uniformly, efficiently, and serenely on an elevated track past Foley's Department Store (now Macy's). (City of Houston Traffic and Transportation Department, People Mover System for Downtown Houston, 1976, and City of Houston, Houston Downtown People Mover: Proposal to the Urban Mass Transit Administration, 1977, Courtesy HMRC, Houston Public Library.)

*Artist rendering showing a close-up of a people mover transit stop located above ground level. (*People Mover System for Downtown Houston, Houston Downtown People Mover, *Courtesy* HMRC, *Houston Public Library.)*

*Aerial view of the people mover and its elevated tracks above Louisiana Street, with a stop at the Hotel Sonesta. It would have been fitting for the Hotel Sonesta to have a people mover stop, since it was designed by famous Los Angeles architect Welton Becket, who designed many of that city's most famous landmarks (the Cinerama Dome, the Capitol Records Building, and the Theme Building at LAX, etc.) and was known for his futuristic vision. (*People Mover System for Downtown Houston, Houston Downtown People Mover, *Courtesy* HMRC, *Houston Public Library.)*

Mall for Second City National Bank (Proposed)

Kenneth Franzheim's far-sighted 1953 proposal for a landscaped pedestrian mall fronting the Second National Bank. Franzheim's recognition of the need for downtown Houston to have more greenery and open space was totally ignored. Portions of the Empire State Plaza in Albany, New York, directly opposite New York's State Capitol, bear a striking resemblance to Franzheim's concept. (Franzheim, Postwar Planning, *Courtesy* HMRC, *Houston Public Library.)*

Entrance to Hermann Park (Proposed)

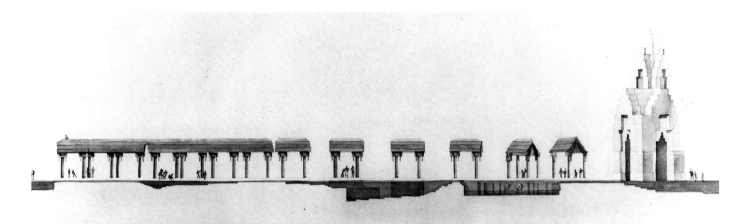

In 1982, Postmodern architect Charles Moore, who was then working with the Urban Innovations Group in Los Angeles, proposed this fanciful row of porticoes to mark the entrance to Hermann Park. The drawing was part of a competition for a much-needed re-vamping of Hermann Park that was supported by the City of Houston's Municipal Arts Commission. Ultimately, no design was ever implemented due to lack of both funding and public support. Two years later, Moore's design for the Wonderwall was constructed for the 1984 New Orleans World's Fair. Moore employed the same serio-comic, kitschy sensibility with the Wonderwall that he had used earlier in his design schemes for Hermann Park. (Charles Moore Collection, Courtesy HMRC, Houston Public Library.)

—— Office Building (Proposed) ——

This twin-towered megalith designed by Alfred Finn in 1927 would have been an impressive addition to Houston's skyline. The design included a pedestrian crosswalk, which can be seen in the rendering linking the two towers near the building's summit. The Petronas Towers in Kuala Lumpur, Malaysia, completed in 1998, were constructed with such a crosswalk, known as a skybridge. (RG E79, Courtesy HMRC, Houston Public Library.)

Miller Summer Auditorium (Proposed)

PROPOSED MILLER SUMMER AUDITORIUM
CITY OF HOUSTON

Kenneth Franzheim submitted this design proposal, ca. 1967, for a new Miller Theater to replace the original classical-style Miller Memorial Theater, designed by William Ward Watkin. Ultimately, Eugene Werlin was selected to design the new theater, which was completed in 1969 and still stands. (Franzheim, Postwar Planning, *Courtesy HMRC, Houston Public Library.)*

— Gulf Building (Proposed) —

An enormous model constructed in Alfred Finn's office showing one of the proposed designs for the Gulf Building, which was completed in 1929 as an Art Deco structure. Had this design been accepted, the skyscraper would have been crowned with an immense cupola. (MSS 19-348, Courtesy HMRC, Houston Public Library.)

Another design proposal from the Finn office for the Gulf Building, much nearer to the design that was ultimately selected. (MSS 19-Job 363, Courtesy HMRC, Houston Public Library.)

The selected design for the Gulf Building, shown after completion in 1929. The Gulf Building was one of several 1920s skyscrapers inspired by Eero Saarinen's second-place design in the competition to design a new headquarters for the Chicago Tribune. *Designed by Finn with the assistance of Kenneth Franzheim and J. E. R. Carpenter, the Gulf Building is widely acknowledged as an Art Deco masterpiece. Today it is known as the J. P. Morgan Chase Tower. (MSS 19-924, Courtesy HMRC, Houston Public Library.)*

—— New Theatre (Proposed) ——

This new theater proposed by Alfred Finn, ca. 1926, would have meant yet another Houston commercial building constructed in the Mediterranean style. Popular in the 1920s, Mediterranean revival was one of the few architectural styles to lend some coherence and uniformity to Houston's cityscape, particularly along Main Street, leading one architectural critic to dub the style "Main Street Mediterranean." (MSS 19-1489, Courtesy HMRC, Houston Public Library.)

Downtown Motor Hotel (Addition to Rice Hotel, Proposed)

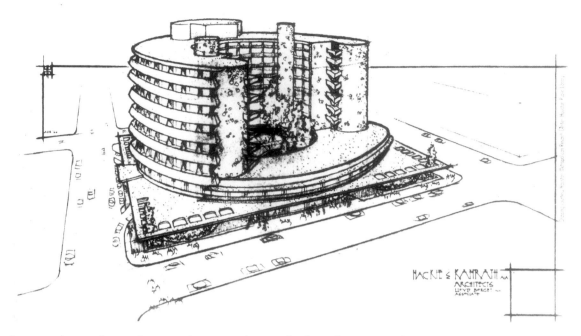

Perspective drawing showing the concept that MacKie & Kamrath submitted in 1960–1961 for a "downtown motor hotel," a proposed addition to the Rice Hotel that would have catered to motor tourists. Almost contemporaneous with the September 1962 premiere of ABC's animated series The Jetsons, *which was set in the twenty-first century, the proposed hotel addition resembles the apartment home of the futuristic Jetson family. (MacKie & Kamrath Collection, Job 60-2322, Courtesy HMRC, Houston Public Library.)*

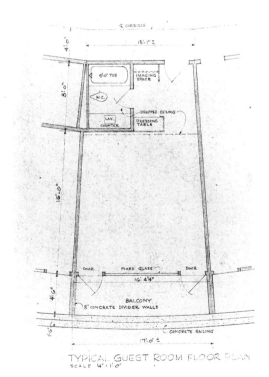

Typical guest room floor plan for the downtown motor hotel by MacKie & Kamrath. (MacKie & Kamrath Collection, Job 60-2322, Courtesy HMRC, Houston Public Library.)

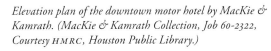

*Elevation plan of the downtown motor hotel by MacKie &
Kamrath. (MacKie & Kamrath Collection, Job 60-2322,
Courtesy HMRC, Houston Public Library.)*

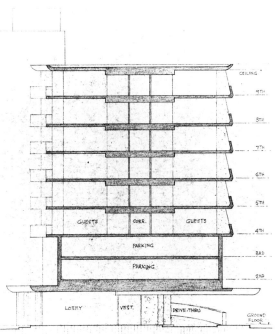

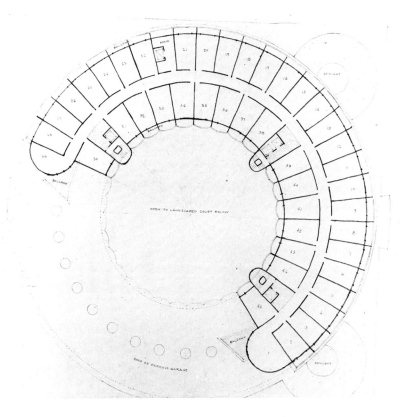

*Typical hotel floor plan by MacKie & Kamrath. (MacKie & Kamrath
Collection, Job 60-2322, Courtesy HMRC, Houston Public Library.)*

Tourist Hotel (Proposed)

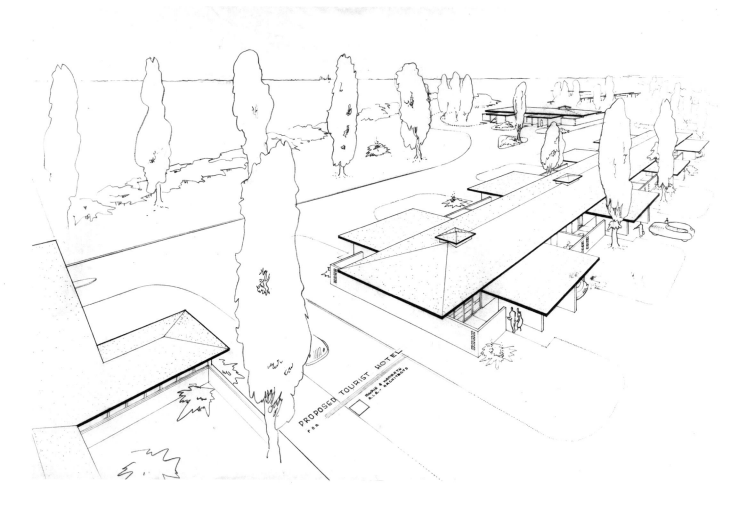

MacKie & Kamrath's 1948 proposal for a tourist hotel would have made an interesting addition to Houston's growing list of Modernist buildings in the late 1940s. The hotel's low-slung, California modern look automatically distinguished it from other contemporary Houston hotels, which were generally high-rises, and was actually more akin to the traditional motel style. (Mackie & Kamrath Collection, Job 46-925, Courtesy HMRC, Houston Public Library.)

UNBUILT HOUSTON

★

[175]

Red Wolf Hotel (Proposed)

"THE RED WOLF"

Well-known commercial architect Kenneth Franzheim came up with this proposal for the Red Wolf Hotel complex for Houston. The hotel's stolid design, complete with setbacks, clearly shows the influence of the years Franzheim worked in New York City, as this proposal would have been equally at home across from Central Park. (Franzheim, Postwar Planning, *Courtesy HMRC, Houston Public Library.)*

Villa Vista Site Plan (Proposed)

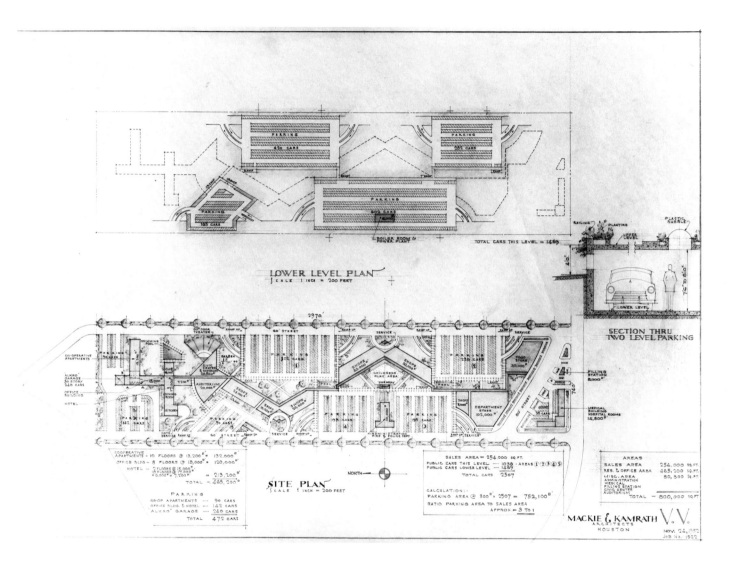

Long before "mixed use" communities became popular, MacKie & Kamrath planned the Vista Villa development, which would have been located just east of the present-day Gulfgate Shopping Center. This "city within a city" featured an underground parking garage with space for nearly 1,500 cars, a ten-story apartment building, a hospital, a civic center and museum, a 102,000-square-foot department store, and a nine-story office building. (MacKie & Kamrath Job 1522, Courtesy Houston Metropolitan Research Center, Houston Public Library.)

Twenty-Story Office Building (Proposed)

SOUTH ELEVATION
SCALE ⅛"=1'-0"

South elevation of MacKie & Kamrath's proposed twenty-story office building, complete with high-rise gardens. Although its architecture was hardly innovative, this would have been only the second skyscraper ever built by MacKie & Kamrath and their first high-rise building in Houston. The firm's first and only skyscraper is the still-extant Pasadena State Bank in Pasadena, Texas. (MacKie & Kamrath Collection, Job 2224-5, Courtesy HMRC, Houston Public Library.)

Apartment House (Proposed)

Rendering of proposed apartment house by Alfred Finn. The design for this stylish Art Moderne apartment house was submitted by Finn in the late 1920s. (MSS 163-0002, Courtesy HMRC, Houston Public Library.)

NOTES

1. Texas Eastern Transmission Corporation, news release, October 11, 1970, Houston Center Vertical File, HMRC.

2. A. de Leon, Texas Eastern Transmission Corporation, memorandum, August 2, 1976, Houston Center Vertical File, HMRC.

3. See also Anderson, "Visions of Monorail in Houston, 1955–1994."

EPILOGUE

Just two weeks after I completed writing the text for *Houston: Lost and Unbuilt*, I read with astonishment that three of the historically important structures I mentioned in the introduction to this book's *Lost Houston* segment—the River Oaks Shopping Center, the River Oaks Theatre, and the Alabama Theatre—were all in danger of being demolished. I had hoped that public outcry over the fate of these buildings might have some chance of reversing, or at least temporarily halting, Houston's frenzy to destroy its past. Unfortunately, these hopes were dashed a short time later in May 2007, when the demolition of the north portion of the River Oaks Shopping Center, one of the earliest shopping centers constructed in this country, began in earnest. One

Aerial view of River Oaks Shopping Center, West Gray at Shepherd, ca. 1937. Despite considerable protests, the property owners demolished the northern portion of the shopping center in 2007 to build a parking garage and Barnes & Noble Store. The auto-oriented center, designed by Stayton Nunn and Milton McGinty, opened in 1937 and was hailed by architects as a model for its progressive design. (Courtesy Bob Bailey Studios Photographic Archive, e_bb_2112, The Center for American History, The University of Texas.)

disheartening story after another regarding the fate of the River Oaks and Alabama theatres soon followed in the *Houston Chronicle* and in newsletters and announcements released by historic preservation groups.

Shockingly, these sad developments were followed in July 2007 by the announcement that nearly all of the buildings in the 800 block of Main Street were soon likely to be demolished to clear the way for a 47-story office building. Among the casualties will be the Beatty-West Building (1912), the Hotel Cotton (1913), and the former Bonds clothing store (1940), which contains unrivaled Art Deco interiors by architect/designer Irving Klein.

A steady succession of announcements of impending or possible demolitions has followed since. Possible casualties include the Lockhart Elementary School (1949), designed by Joseph Finger and George Rustay; Kenneth Franzheim's downtown YMCA building (1941); and yet another proposal in October 2008 for reuse of the Astrodome. This time, the domed stadium would become the Astrodome Studios, a gigantic movie production facility. Like earlier proposals, the Dome's exterior would remain intact, but the historic interior design would be destroyed.

Shortly before demolition of a portion of the River Oaks Shopping Center began, the Houston City Council proceeded to designate all three of these buildings as City of Houston Landmarks. Under the provisions of the City's preservation ordinance, first passed in 1995 and expanded in 2005, even after buildings are designated by the city as historic properties, the owners/developers can apply for a certificate of nondesignation, which delays the formal designation for six months, allowing ample time to demolish the structure in the interim. In September 2008, the director of Houston's Historic Neighborhoods Council acknowledged that the creation of historic districts, intended to help preserve entire neighborhoods rather than individual structures, "has done nothing to stop the tide of demolition in these neighborhoods."[1]

Does this really represent what a *New York Times* reporter described in 2006 as "drawing a rare line in the sand in defense of some particularly beloved architectural treasures?"[2] If so, Houston can and must do better in saving its historic built environment. Such lines in the sand have been drawn and redrawn in the past, and each line is quickly wiped away. However, despite the many setbacks in the struggle to save Houston's architectural heritage, I hope I have helped to introduce a change in this outlook, and I hope it is a change in outlook that many more Houstonians will come to share with me as well as with Houston's small, but determined historic preservation community.

NOTES

1. Courtney Tardy, "From the HNC Director," *Historic Neighborhoods Council eNewsletter*, September 2008.
2. Ralph Blumenthal, "Fighting the Wrecking Ball to Save Houston Landmarks," *New York Times*, August 12, 2006.

BIBLIOGRAPHY

Anderson, Brian. "Visions of Monorail in Houston, 1955–1994," *Houston Review* 17, no. 1 (1995): 29–48.

Architectural Collections. Houston Metropolitan Research Center. Houston Public Library, Houston, TX.

Arenas, Reinaldo. *Before Night Falls.* New York: InsideOut Books, 2001.

Benson, Timothy, O. *Expressionist Utopias.* Los Angeles: Los Angeles County Museum of Art, 1993.

Berman, Marshall. *All That Is Solid Melts into Air: The Experience of Modernity.* New York: Simon and Schuster, 1982.

Bob Bailey Studios Photographic Archive. The Center for American History, The University of Texas at Austin. Austin, TX.

Botton, Alain de. *The Architecture of Happiness.* New York: Pantheon Books, 2006.

Boym, Svetlana. *The Future of Nostalgia.* New York: Basic Books, 2001.

Brosterman, Norman. *Out of Time: Designs for the Twentieth-Century Future.* New York: Harry N. Abrams, Inc., 2000.

Calvino, Italo. *Invisible Cities.* New York: Harcourt Books, 1974.

Casebere, James, and Glen Seator. *The Architectural Unconscious.* Andover, MA: Addison Gallery of American Art, 2000.

City Book of Houston. Houston, TX: Rein & Sons Co., 1925.

Collins, George R. *Visionary Drawings of Architecture and Planning: 20th Century through the 1960s.* Cambridge, MA: MIT Press, 1979.

Courtney, Linda Anderson. "The Evolution of Cinema Design in Houston, 1900–1920," *Houston Review* 4, no. 1 (1983): 28–43.

Davis, Howard. *The Culture of Building,* Oxford: Oxford UP, 2006.

Dickey, George, Collection. Houston Metropolitan Research Center. Houston Public Library, Houston, TX.

Ferris, Hugh, and Carol Willis. *The Metropolis of Tomorrow.* New York: Princeton Architectural Press, 1986.

Finn, Alfred, Collection. Houston Metropolitan Research Center. Houston Public Library, Houston, TX.

Fox, Stephen. *Houston Architectural Guide.* 2nd ed. AIA and Herring Press, 1999.

Franzheim, Kenneth. *Postwar Planning: Houston.* n.p., 1946.

GHPA. Greater Houston Preservation Alliance Web site. www.ghpa.org.

———. *Houston Deco: Modernistic Architecture of the Texas Coast.* www.houstondeco.org.

Hadley, Nancy, and Steven R. Strom. "Innovation, Boosterism, and Agriculture on the Gulf Coast, 1890–1920," *Houston Review* 14, no. 2 (1992): 103–121.

Hare & Hare Collection. Houston Metropolitan Research Center. Houston Public Library, Houston, TX.

Heinzelman, Kurt, ed. *Make It New: The Rise of Modernism.* Austin, TX: The University of Texas Press, 2003.

Historic Houston. Historic Houston: Sustainable Building Resources. www.historichouston.org.

Houston Post (Supplement). "Houston Tomorrow: Leaders Project City Into the Year 2000," February 9, 1964.

Houston Public Library. "First Report and Resume of the History of the Houston Lyceum and Carnegie Library Association to the Mayor and City Council, 1904." Houston, TX: n.p., 1904.

Huxtable, Ada Louise. "Deep in the Heart of Nowhere," *New York Times,* February 15, 1976.

Klein, Norman M. *The History of Forgetting: Los Angeles and the Erasure of Memory.* New York: Verso Press, 1997.

Kreneck, Thomas. *Del Pueblo: A Pictorial History of Houston's Hispanic Community.* Houston, TX: Houston International University, 1989.

Lent, Joy. *Houston's Heritage: Using Antique Postcards.* Houston, TX: D. H. White, 1983.

Litterst-Dixon Collection. Houston Metropolitan Research Center. Houston Public Library, Houston, TX.

Loewy, Raymond. *Never Leave Well Enough Alone.* New York: Simon and Schuster, 1951.

Lohren, Olle, Collection. Houston Metropolitan Research Center. Houston Public Library, Houston, TX.

Lowenthal, David. *The Heritage Crusade and the Spoils of History.* Cambridge: Cambridge University Press, 1996.

———. *The Past is a Foreign Country.* Cambridge: Cambridge University Press, 1985.

MacKie & Kamrath Collection. Houston Metropolitan Research Center. Houston Public Library, Houston, TX.

Marshall, Alex. *How Cities Work: Suburbs, Sprawl, and the Roads Not Taken.* Austin, TX: University of Texas Press, 2003.

Moore, Barry. "Better Off Without It: The 1910 Municipal Auditorium," *Cite: The Architecture and Design Review of Houston* 62 (Fall 2004).

Norberg-Schultz, Christian. *Principles of Modern Architecture.* London: Andreas Papadrakis Publisher, 2000.

Papademetriou, Peter C. *Houston: An Architectural Guide.* Houston, TX: American Institute of Architects, 1972.

Pfeiffer, Bruce Brooks. *Frank Lloyd Wright: His Living Voice.* Fresno, CA: The Press at California State University, 1987.

The Red Book of Houston: A Compendium of Social, Professional, Religious, Educational and Industrial Interests of Houston's Colored Population. Houston, TX: Sotex Publishing, 1915.

Scardino, Barrie. "A Legacy of Houston City Halls," *Houston Review* 5, no. 3 (1982): 155–163.

Sky, Alison, and Michelle Stone. *Unbuilt America: Forgotten Architecture in the United States from Thomas Jefferson to the Space Age.* New York: Abbeville Press, 1976.

Southwest Center for Urban Research and the School of Architects. *Houston Architectural Survey* (6 vols.), Houston: Rice University, 1980–1981.

Strom, Steven R. "A Chronicle of Houston's History: Twenty Years of Architectural Records at the Houston Public Library," *Houston Review* 19, no. 2 (1997) 19–28.

———. "The Houston That Never Was," *Cite: The Architecture and Design Review of Houston* 50 (Fall 2004): 30–33.

———. "A Legacy of Civic Pride: Houston's PWA Buildings," *Houston Review* 17, no. 2 (1995).

———. "Lost Houston: Images from a Century of Erasure," *Cite: The Architecture and Design Review of Houston* 46 (Fall 1999–Winter 2000): 21–29.

———, ed. *MacKie & Kamrath Architects: Guide to the Architectural Collection.* Houston, TX: Houston Public Library, 2000.

———. "Modernism for the Masses," *Cite: The Architecture and Design Review of Houston* 62 (Fall 2004): 30–33.

Texas State Historical Association, Handbook of Texas Online, http://www.tshaonline.org/handbook/online/index.html.

Thomas, Jesse O. *A Study of the Social Welfare Status of the Negroes in Houston, Texas.* Houston, Texas: Webster-Richardson Publishing Co., Inc., 1929.

van Schaik, Leon. Introduction to *Melbourne's Unseen Might-Have Beens Exhibition: Unbuilt Projects Catalogue.* Victoria, Aus.: Royal Australian Institute of Architecture, 1987.

Vertical File Collections. Houston Metropolitan Research Center. Houston Public Library, Houston, TX.

Webb, Bruce. "The Name Game," *Cite: The Architecture and Design Review of Houston* 46 (Fall 1999–Winter 2000): 16–20.

Welling, David. *Cinema Houston: From Nickelodeon to Megaplex.* Austin, TX: University of Texas Press, 2007.

Wilson, Michael E., ed. *Alfred C. Finn: Builder of Houston.* Houston: Houston Public Library, 1983.

Winchester, Simon. *A Crack in the Edge of the World: America and the Great California Earthquake of 1906.* New York: Harper Collins, 2005.

INDEX